AF254854

Soul Plan, Contracts, and Trap

Unlocking Ancient Wisdom through Numerology, Astrology, and the Akashic Records to Uncover Humanity's Forgotten Potential

Your Free Gift
(only available for a limited time)

Thanks for getting this book! If you want to learn more about various spirituality topics, then join Mari Silva's community and get a free guided meditation MP3 for awakening your third eye. This guided meditation mp3 is designed to open and strengthen ones third eye so you can experience a higher state of consciousness. Simply visit the link below the image to get started.

https://spiritualityspot.com/meditation

Or, Scan the QR code!

Table of Contents

Part 1: Soul Plan and Soul Contracts

Decode Your Soul's Mission Through Numerology, Astrology, Akashic Records, Spiritual Communication, and Secret Wisdom

Introduction

Everyone has wondered, at least once, if there was more to life than what meets the eye – if there was a point to every encounter and every happenstance.

Why do bad things happen? Why do good things happen? Is there a grand plan or purpose guiding your steps, even if you can't always see them? The concepts of soul contracts and soul plans sound a bit esoteric. However, whether you believe in them or not, they're thought-provoking and could show you a few things about your soul's mission on earth – why you're here.

The book title caught your attention, so perhaps you have a basic understanding of soul contracts, or deep down, you know there's more to this existence than what everyone else sees on the surface. There's a pull, a yearning to find and follow the elusive threads found throughout time and, of course, your life – and this book will help you understand it all.

A soul contract is a proposal, an agreement you made with your higher self before you were born. This contract contains the lessons, relationships, and experiences you committed to exploring in this lifetime. And your soul plan? It's the navigational system or compass that helps you fulfill the contract.

Why does life feel so complicated sometimes if all this planning was done beforehand?

If you're contemplating this, then you're asking the right questions. In this book, you'll learn the nature of soul-level agreements, how to identify your contract's major components, how to work with your energy, and how to align with your soul's highest intentions.

Many books are available on this topic. However, you may find their approach a little dry or academic. But not with this book. You'll notice a more hands-on, interactive feel that teaches you to establish a better connection between you and your spiritual self than ever before.

You won't need two books to understand the twin concepts of soul contracts and soul plans. Not when everything you need is right here, in one thoughtfully crafted volume. Both concepts are inextricably linked, and when you understand the big picture, the *"why"* of your life experiences, the cycles, joys, and hardships, they form part of a conscious, divinely engineered display with you at the center.

Chapter 1: Understanding Soul Contracts and Pre-Birth Agreements

It is believed that long before you took your first breath, your soul – the eternal, non-physical you – went through intense, meticulous preparation. You sat down (metaphorically) with your higher self, spiritual guides, and other souls you're destined to meet and devised a plan for your journey to Earth. This is called a soul contract.

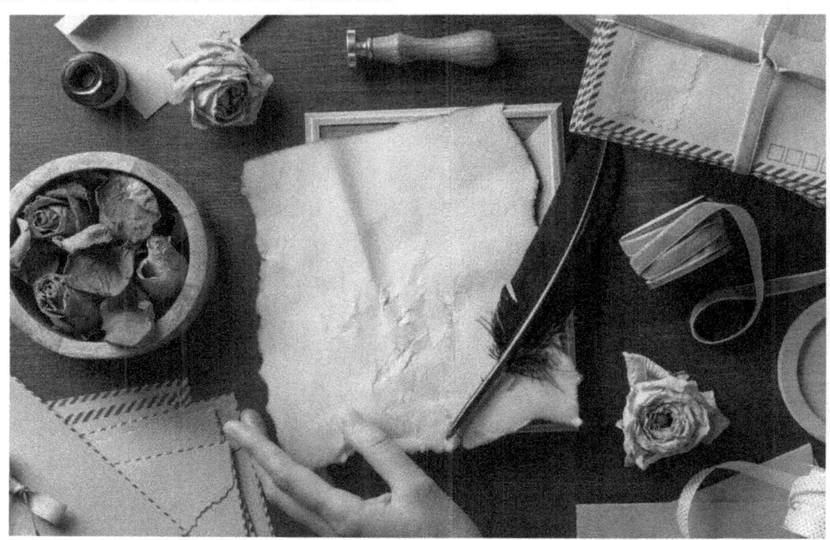

Soul contracts are energetic agreements.[1]

Soul contracts are energetic agreements made before incarnating into this physical plane. Before you run away screaming at the thought of more paperwork, soul-level agreements are not the legalese you'd find in a standard contract. They are cosmic, a divine to-do list of your higher self noted from pure inspiration. The language is direct, the terms are non-negotiable (at least by your ego), and there's not a single clause about late fees.

Humans overcomplicate things. However, your higher self operates on a different frequency with access to the big picture. They can see your journey's perfect map from that expansive vantage point – the necessary relationships, lessons, and opportunities that will catalyze a rebirth, your transformation. Knowing what they know, they drafted your soul contract, complete with every ingredient you need to accomplish your soul's destiny.

Things get complicated once you incarnate and get absorbed into hustle culture.

Many things are required daily, including many societal constructs that you must abide by as a member of society. As expected, you forget about your pre-planned agreements at birth, and life has a way of burying your destiny underneath the rubble of human existence. Your ego takes over, and you are led astray from your soul's true purpose. Luckily, your higher self anticipated this. They knew you'd get swept up in the chaos the moment you opened your eyes. They saw it coming – the drama, the social obligations, and the intrusive thoughts – but won't leave things to chance. They're always one step ahead and built-in little breadcrumbs and trail markers to help guide you back to your soul's true path.

Suppose you get these nagging feelings or inexplicable connections with certain people. In that case, it's a part of your soul contract being activated. You may have a friend you've known since you were in diapers, and don't talk to them anymore, but never delete their number. Or maybe there's one coworker who gets under your skin, for better or worse. Or you've experienced an inescapable pull towards a person, even when logic says you should be running in the other direction? How many times have you met someone and felt an immediate connection, like you've known them for lifetimes? More often than not, these are manifestations of your soul contract.

When you open your eyes to the divine orchestration of your relationships and life story, the irritating tension with your younger sister is no longer pointless drama but an opportunity to learn patience. That dead-end job you got fired from could be your reminder to stop settling and chase your dreams. Regardless of whether it has been scientifically proven, this perspective takes you out of a victim mentality and redirects you to find meaning and clarity in your life.

The Purpose of Soul Contracts

- **Lessons**: A guru or shaman will tell you that this is the real reason we're all here. Your soul contract is a personalized curriculum tailored only for you. They lead you to and through good and bad experiences necessary for your consciousness's growth and expansion.

- **Karmic Balancing**: Karma . . . the cosmic IOU that keeps on giving, right? Through your soul contracts, you can settle outstanding karmic debts or relationships from your past lives. You can forgive and be forgiven by those you've previously crossed paths with. You get a do-over, although what you do with it is ultimately your choice.

- **Soul Purpose Alignment**: Your soul purpose covers everything you are meant to do in this lifetime. It is the path your soul is destined to follow. Your soul contract puts up signposts on this path to keep you en route. This route should take you to the people, places, and encounters that will help you fulfill your divine calling and become the highest version of yourself.

Your soul purpose is to find the right path.[2]

- **Relationship Dynamics**: Your soul contract stipulates the connections you'll have with the important people in your life. These connections can be a karmic bond to a romantic soulmate. They create the conditions for the lessons you'll learn together and the resulting growth experiences.

- **Spiritual Transformation**: Despite what is written in your soul contract, you have free will. You can choose not to honor your contract's details. However, if you live in alignment with it, you're essentially inviting the universe to shake your foundations. Your entire life goes from black-and-white to full-blown technicolor, and it is the most beautiful yet bittersweet experience. All roads lead to your soul's purpose. You can ignore the directions and carve your own path. Still, soul contract coordinates exist for a reason that you will only understand if you follow them.

The Elements of a Soul Contract

- **Birth and Early Life Experiences:** The circumstances surrounding your birth- such as the time, location, and family into which you are born- are intentionally chosen and stipulated in your soul contract. Childhood experiences, including your family relationship, traumas, or significant events, are intentional because they shape your personality, emotional patterns, and karmic lessons.

- **Karmic Lessons:** Karmic lessons are major themes or lessons your soul has agreed to work through during this lifetime. These lessons are usually based on unresolved issues or imbalances from your past lives, which you've brought forward to address and eventually transcend. They are not pretty, but that's usually the point, or you may never confront your fears and learn the lessons.

- **Karmic Relationships:** These are the connections you agreed to revisit in this lifetime to work through lingering issues, heal old wounds, and, most importantly, shed negative patterns. Relationships like these are intense, charged, and hardly ever peaceful. They conjure your deepest fears, insecurities, and triggers – what you need to confront and integrate to break free from the cycle of karma.

- **Soulmate Connections:** When people think of soulmates, they immediately consider a romantic partnership with two people who fit together in a way that makes sense. They're not wrong. However, soulmate connections can show up in other forms, like a best friend, a role model, family, or a familiar stranger. There's always recognition, understanding, and resonance between soulmates, regardless of their form. You feel like you've known this person for ages, even if you've just met them. There's an effortless flow to the relationship, an intuitive communication beyond words. While not karmic, these relationships will test you, push you out of your comfort zone, or reveal parts of yourself that you've kept hidden.

- **Tests of Faith and Perseverance:** Life will test you. There's no need to sugarcoat it. There will be periods of uncertainty that test your persistence, patience, and strength of character. However intense they may feel, these tests are not random or arbitrary. They are carefully designed teaching moments put on your path to help you transcend old limitations and stretch the boundaries of your consciousness. It is part of the grand, multidimensional syllabus you signed up for.

Pre-Birth Agreements

Before you were incarnated on this planet, you existed somewhere else, as pure consciousness, in a non-physical, spiritual place. This version of you is your higher self. It was here, in this formless state, where you intentionally plotted the parameters of the life that you were about to undertake on the physical plane. It was here that you thought of the main narrative arc, character development, and important themes of your storyline.

A significant part of this pre-birth process is establishing soul agreements, pacts you make with other souls who have important roles in your future life. These pacts could be contracts with family members, lovers, close friends, mentors, or rivals. They create the relationships and exchanges that form the optimal conditions for your spiritual growth and fulfillment of your soul's agenda.

Your soul agreements aren't rigid or set in stone because, within the agreements, you have free will. You're not doomed to have a difficult relationship with everyone you enter a soul agreement with. For example, your rivals or enemies aren't necessarily there to drive you crazy. They might, but that's not the point. They may have agreed to play that role to force you out of your comfort zone, trigger epiphanies, or push you to address lingering inner conflicts. Regardless, how you respond to these people and situations is up to you.

Another pre-birth agreement involves your relationship with your physical vessel – your body. Your soul carefully selects the genetic, energetic, and circumstantial makeup of its human form. Factors like your gender, ethnicity, natural talents, and weaknesses – and even the time and place of your birth – are consciously chosen to serve the soul's evolutionary agenda. Your body is the vehicle that carries your soul through this lifetime, so your soul puts a lot of thought and intention into selecting the right form for its mission. Your body is a manifestation of your soul's intentions.

Outside the agreements you make with the souls incarnating with you, your higher self actively seeks out ascended masters, angelic guides, and other highly evolved consciousnesses to guide and support you. They are your spirit guides. This invisible network is always available, whether or not you're aware of its presence. They have access to perspectives and knowledge transcending the physical world. When you open yourself to their guidance, you receive signs and synchronicities that point you in the right direction.

Interplanetary and Extraterrestrial Pre-Birth Agreements

Your astrological birth chart might tell you which and where planets were at the time of your birth. However, the soul agreements you made prior to incarnation include more than the celestial bodies in the solar system. Your soul contract carries the fingerprints of other planetary and star systems.

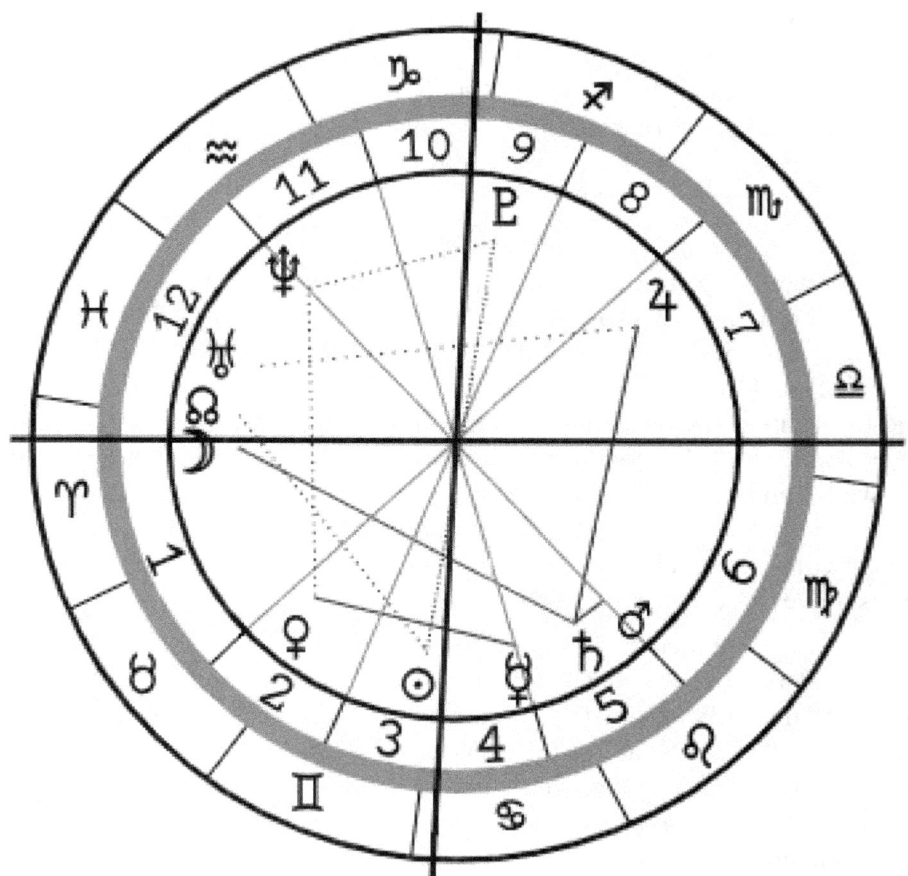

Birth charts can tell you about your alignment with the universe.'

Every person has the same elements created in the belly of dying stars billions of years ago that have been found in everything on Earth. Science has proven this. You are, in essence, a child of the universe.

Some people feel a strong, mysterious connection to ancient Sumerian symbols or lunar cycles or something well beyond the solar system. These could be signs that their soul's pre-birth agreements involve close ties to planetary archetypes and star systems far outside Earth. Best-selling author and medical intuitive Caroline Myss explained that the energetic imprints of celestial bodies, including ones far away, can reveal much about your soul's evolutionary journey. For example, those with strong Sirian influences might feel called to teaching roles, wisdom-sharing, and humanitarian service. Whereas Venusian energies may find expression through artistry, beauty, and loving relationships. Arcturians are known for being gifted healers, peacemakers, and pioneers of cutting-edge spiritual technologies. While these are not rigidly deterministic, and many people could have ties to more than one-star system, it doesn't hurt to ask, "What do I feel called to?"

Choice and Destiny

Since humanity can recall, philosophers, theologians, and ordinary people have racked their brains for answers to the age-old question: Does free will exist, or is life predetermined by a higher power or force? Is fate a matter of choice or destiny? These questions are deep, complex, and perennial. The implications of how they are answered can irrevocably alter human's understanding of life, purpose, and place in the universe. If there is true free will, then you bear responsibility for your actions and the trajectory of your life. However, if everything is predetermined, then how much control does anyone genuinely have? Are people merely puppets dancing to the forces that eclipse comprehension?

Weighty existential quandaries like these can tie anyone's brain into knots, and the older you get, the more complicated and mind-boggling they become. When you were nine, the answers were clear-cut. "Duh! I have free will. I do what I want every day." Then life comes at you, and setbacks set in. Tragedies and unanticipated redirections make you question whether you're in the driver's seat. Life is like the old saying, "We plan, and God laughs."

Choice implies agency, the capacity to decide and direct the course of your life. Whenever you choose, you exercise free will – the power to select options and do only what you want. Free will suggests that the future is not set in stone but malleable based on your choices in the present.

Alternatively, destiny insinuates a predetermined fate or course of events completely out of your control. It means there is a higher power, God, the universe, or another force that has already mapped out your entire life. So, no matter what choices you think you're making, you are only playing out a script that has already been written. Your life stops being the product of your volition. It is the unfolding of a plan set in motion long before your parents were born.

So, Which Is It, Choice or Destiny?

According to many spiritual and philosophical traditions, the answer is in the soul's flexibility and intentionality. The soul is not bound by rigid destiny but instead returns to life with specific experiences and lessons it hopes to experiment with and master. Despite this, the soul maintains the freedom of how it responds to those experiences.

Is life about choice, destiny, or both?[4]

In the video game *Detroit: Become Human*, you follow the stories of three humanoid androids in a futuristic timeline where artificial intelligence has developed self-awareness and emotions. Despite their programming to fulfill certain functions, these androids soon figure out that they can make choices that determine their lives and the course of human-android relations. This game has multiple endings, each determined by the choices you, the player, make.

This reference explains the symbiotic relationship between predetermination and free will. You may feel bound by your genetic programming, upbringing, or societal conditioning, but your capacity for conscious choice and free will defines who you are and what you become.

Will you surrender to your base impulses? Will you give in to fear at every turn? Will you rise above the limitations of your circumstances? You own a good portion of the responsibility for the choices you make. You can't always blame your genes, childhood, or culture for your outcomes. The buck stops with you. You are your story's author, come what may. So, what will you do with the gift of free will?

Choosing Your Destiny

Everyone knows about intuition. However, no one, not even science, has figured out how it works. You know why it works but not necessarily how. Essentially, intuition is rapid, unconscious information processing. The brain can draw upon past experiences, accumulated knowledge, and muted environmental cues to produce or inspire quick insights and hunches – typically before you're even consciously aware. Picture your mind as an iceberg. The conscious, logical mind is only the tip, while the majority of your mental activity happens below the surface, subconsciously. Intuition originates from this subconscious database filled with stored information and pattern recognition, which is how you make snap judgments and decisions without understanding their full rationale.

Your mind is like an iceberg, with visible and invisible traits.[5]

Humans aren't the only ones who possess intuition. Birds know when to migrate. A dog senses danger before its owner does. A dolphin can detect sickness. A Border Collie knows how to herd animals. How? They can't tell you, but these are examples of intuition in action. Humans are only as instinctive as animals in the animal kingdom but ignore or distrust that part of themselves in favor of their logical, rational minds.

Intuition is the soul's preferred method of communication. Not everyone can always consciously articulate the reasoning behind their intuitive hunches. However, those gut feelings are direct communications from the subconscious mind, and that part of you is aware of your soul contract and the unfolding of your soul's journey.

You have free will, but you can use this free will in alignment with your soul's mission – a mission you are being guided to intuitively. The more you trust your intuitive wisdom, the easier it becomes to discern between the authentic choices of your soul and those driven by more superficial, egoic impulses. Not all your hunches will be intuitive. Sometimes it's fear or anxiety. You can separate wisdom from your ego's chatter *and* live in sync with your destiny, *and* co-create your life in partnership with your soul's higher intelligence with meditation, mindfulness, and other spiritual practices.

Questionnaire: Understand Your Soul Contract

1. What are the predominant themes or patterns consistently showing up in your life despite the changes or transitions you go through? These should point you to potential lessons or soul-level agreements for this lifetime.

   ____

   ____

   ____

   ____

   ____

   ____

   ____

2. Are there particular situations or problems you repeatedly deal with, even if the details are different? Maybe you keep dating the same types of people, even when you choose a different "type," or you keep trading one addiction for another. These could be the manifestation of unfinished business within your soul contract. Answer:

3. Are there recurring emotional states, behaviors, or thought patterns that refuse to leave you alone?

4. What are the foundational values, beliefs, or principles that have been steady guides for your choices?

5. Consider the relationships that matter the most to you. They could be your boyfriend, girlfriend, spouse, best friend, family, etc. Are there common themes between them? If yes, what are they?

6. Are there specific archetypes or roles people always play in your life, even if they have nothing in common? For example, are your friends always the caretaking, authoritarian, or defiant types?

7. Looking back at your relationships, what lessons do you think you were meant to learn? Is there a major lesson those relationships were trying to teach you?

8. Do the issues in your relationships mirror the internal work you need to do? How?

9. When you think about the biggest transitions and turning points in your life, what are the common themes?

____

____

____

____

____

____

____

10. Are there particular character archetypes, symbols, or motifs that recur in your life and dreams? It could be more than one. Archetypes are categories for characters representing universal traits or ideas that are easily recognizable. Character archetypes include the wounded healer, the trickster, the magician, the sage, and the orphan.

____

____

____

____

____

____

____

11. How do these archetypal energies and themes relate to the lessons you think you're here to learn?

____

____

____

____

____

____

____

12. How are these themes and archetypes expressed in your outer life?
How are they expressed in your psychological and spiritual
environment?

13. What are the most persistent problems in your life?

14. Do you think these problems are related to your growth and
purpose? How?

15. In what area of your life do you feel stuck? Where can you identify
the most resistance? Is it in your career, finances, health, self-image,
or self-expression?

____

16. What lessons must you master to free yourself from these
blockages?

____

Chapter 2: What Is My Purpose?

From the wealthiest person in your neighborhood to the homeless guy down the street, everyone wants to feel that their lives are fulfilling and have meaning. This search for meaning and fulfillment is a universal human desire, but it's also highly personal to each person. What does it mean to live a fulfilling life? What is meaningful and fulfilling in life? Meaning leads to a purposeful life. A meaningful life contributes value to the world, and fulfillment signifies contentment, satisfaction, and self-actualization. The two are closely linked, yet it's possible to have one without the other. Some people find their lives meaningful but not especially fulfilling. Others may feel fulfilled but struggle to pinpoint the greater meaning of their lives.

What does a meaningful life consist of?[6]

Isn't it easier to live life freely without a concern for what the point is? Where does this drive for meaning and fulfillment come from? Some say it's the intrinsic human need for connection, importance, and transcendence. Humans are social creatures who love belonging and feel a strong need to affect their environment somehow. People are hardwired to ponder the big questions of existence – why are we here, what is the nature of consciousness, is there a higher power or higher purpose? The answers involve a lot of self-reflection, experimentation, and trial and error. Some turn to religion or spirituality, hoping to find meaning through faith and connection to the divine. Some find meaning in their work, relationships, creativity, or service to people. Others feel stuck with existential angst, not knowing if there is any true meaning to be found.

Searching for More

It's not always easy to differentiate between genuine spiritual or existential longing and restlessness or boredom. Today, society rewards productivity and material success above all else, so admitting to this need for purpose can feel like admitting weakness. Still, the search for meaning has inspired the greatest works of art, scientific discoveries, and some of the world's most influential philosophies and religions. Do you know your purpose? How can you be sure that your life isn't meaningful or fulfilling? How do you know you are searching for more?

The most common signs are:

• Restlessness and Dissatisfaction

This comes with a dull sense that something is missing, even when your life looks generally successful or comfortable. You could be daydreaming about quitting your job or fed up with the daily grind. Persistent dissatisfaction is usually a sign that your soul is searching for something more meaningful and in line with your calling and values. You can push these feelings aside all you want and tell yourself to be grateful for what you have. However, it doesn't change the truth about what your soul wants.

• Repetitive Daydreams

Sometimes, your mind wonders about alternative lives or missed opportunities. However, when these daydreams refuse to go away, you may need to pay attention. What are your imagination's themes? Are you fantasizing about fame, a specific industry, spending more time with friends, or a radical shift in how you spend your time? Your repetitive daydreams might be breadcrumbs leading you to your purpose.

- ### • Lack of Meaning and Purpose

In the many components that constitute your life – your work, relationships, pastimes, and daily routine – do you find meaning and purpose? Or are they more of a means to an end, a way to get through the day? As you can guess, mundane activities can be filled with much meaning if they give your life purpose. On the other hand, if your life feels like mindless repetition, it may be time to reevaluate what you think your purpose is.

- ### • Flow and Timelessness

Do you remember the last time you were so absorbed in an activity that you didn't notice time zooming by? What were you doing? Were you singing, painting, coding, or out with your best friends? Losing time in mid-activity means you were in the flow state. When you're in this zone, your enthusiasm and concentration become effortless. If you don't have activities where you can lose yourself, you may be lacking in purpose.

- ### • The Desire to Make a Positive Change

Many people want to leave a positive legacy. They want their lives to matter; they want to contribute something meaningful to their community and the world. You may feel the same way. You're drawn to causes, organizations, or lifestyles for a palpable effect because you desire a purpose.

- ### • Spiritual or Existential Curiosity

For many, the search for more is directly tied to meaning, purpose, and the truth about existence. It's the big question: Why are we here? What happens when we die? Is God real? Curiosity about the universe's mysteries has led many to contemplate philosophies, religions, or paths to self-discovery in the pursuit of answers and their purpose.

What Is My Purpose?

Nobody's purpose is neatly packaged and presented to them on a silver platter or a fixed destination. There will always be something to discover about who you are and what you have to offer the world if you are patient, curious, and willing to figure it out. In most cases, the initial impulse is to look outward – to look for purpose in work, your roles, or your effect on the environment. Undoubtedly, there's value in that. When you feel your life is making a meaningful contribution through your career, volunteering, or raising a family, it feels like your life means something. However, the search for purpose requires looking inward, too. Who are you? What do you value? What are you afraid of? Outside what society has labeled success, what makes you truly happy?

Purpose doesn't have to be grand or earth-shattering. Sometimes, it's as small as kindness, creativity, or presence - the parent working tirelessly to give their child the world, the artist who communicates through their art, the kind soul working in hospice. An ordinary life can have an extraordinary meaning.

Purpose isn't static or singular. It is bound to shift and change as you move through different stages of life. What felt meaningful in your 20s may feel different in your 40s or 60s. You grew, so you should adapt. You're not the same person you were five or ten years ago. Your priorities have shifted. Your purpose is inseparably linked to personal growth and evolution. As you mature and become more experienced, your perspective on what matters may expand or change entirely. No, you haven't gone out of alignment with your soul. You're unfolding gradually and beautifully, like a flower. What seems different and out of alignment might be that you are *more in alignment* than ever before.

Becoming aligned could mean disorientation, uncertainty, and existential crisis. You may question everything you believe. You may doubt your choices and get lost in the maze of life. However, if you are strong enough to sit in the discomfort, do what you must, and trust the process, you will realize that your soul is taking you precisely where you must be.

Autonomy and Self-Determination

The 21st century is marked by technological advancement, global interconnectedness, and the domination of large institutions threatening autonomy and self-determination, *whether people admit it or not.* Every day, you are assaulted with messages from the media, advertisers, corporations, friends, and family, telling you how you should live. There's so much pressure to conform, climb the corporate ladder, and get rich no matter what it takes at the cost of your values, even if the cost is yourself.

Society is slowly but surely inching toward a hive-mind mentality as more people lose touch with their freedom, intuitive wisdom, and authentic self-expression. The temptation to just go along with it and avoid rocking the boat is so strong, especially when the consequences of bucking the system are public shunning and physical threats. Is it possible to balance free will and a soul contract when the cultural narrative is hell-bent on conformity and compliance? The answer is absolutely.

Society is now living with a hive-mind mentality.[7]

The human soul is wired for freedom – freedom to express, to create, and to be. Your free will isn't an accessory to humanity. It is the foundation upon which your soul contract rests. Your soul contract requires active, conscious participation because the more you cede your directorial control to outside forces, the more the vision gets diluted, and the point gets lost.

You may be drawn to a random book or podcast for no apparent reason, only to discover that their message is precisely what you need to hear. You get an idea or inspiration that feels like it was downloaded into your brain from outside of your conscious mind. Or someone gives you something seemingly useless that you need at the next minute.

The orchestrated perfection is unmistakable when living in attunement with these discreet, energetic signals. Things that felt like a mere coincidence or random chance become a puzzle piece to a more intelligent design. You can no longer deny that everything is happening for you, not to you, and helping you manifest your highest purpose.

All you have to do is commit to honoring your truth and walking the road less traveled. In recognition of your courage, the universe responds in kind, opening doors, manufacturing possibilities, and sending you the people, resources, and wisdom you need when you need them most. When you're aligned with your soul's purpose, you can trust that there's a method to the madness, even if you can't see it yet.

Tools and Practices for Uncovering Your Purpose

Boredom Is Not Always Bad

Boredom has become a dirty word. Every minute must be filled with stimulation, doom scrolling on social media, binge-watching TV shows, and rushing from one obligation to the next. The slight prospect of being alone with your thoughts for more than a few minutes fills many with nameless dread.

Modern life is frenetic. People are so overstimulated that they've forgotten how to listen to themselves. There is always a distraction. It's your phone notifications going crazy or the many "must-dos" on your to-do list causing your soul's still, small voice to get drowned out. More people need to intentionally make space for stillness and silence if there is a hope of giving that small voice a chance to be heard. It's in the emptiness when you suppress the impulse to reach for your phone or turn on the TV that you hear what your soul is telling you.

This is a tough sell in today's restless, productivity-obsessed culture, conditioned to see idleness as a moral failing, a wasted opportunity, and a problem to solve. What's the worst thing that could happen if there was nothing but you and silence? What if it holds the answers you seek about who you are, why you're here, and how you're meant to serve?

Journaling

The thought of sitting down to write in a journal is scary, the fear reserved for homework and office presentations. Who would think that the answer to "What is my purpose?" could be at the bottom of a pen?

Journaling can open the windows to your soul.[8]

Contrary to popular opinion, writing in a journal is not stuffy or rigid. It can be wonderfully fluid and creative. Write down your thoughts, even the *"dumb"* ones. Write down your dreams, especially those you're too afraid to tell anyone. Write down your wishes, particularly those that feel so out of reach. Write it all down. Don't think too much about the wording, if it's organized, or if it makes sense. Your journal is a mirror. Only one pair of eyes is staring into it, yours. Nobody else is looking. What do you like? What don't you like? What happened yesterday, and how did it make you feel? Pick any of the following prompts and see where it takes you:

1. Describe your perfect day from start to finish.
2. What are you most grateful for right now?
3. Make a list of 10 things that make you happy.
4. Write about a childhood memory that makes you smile.
5. If you could travel anywhere in the world, where would you go? Why?
6. What are your biggest fears? Do you think you can get over them? How?
7. Describe your dream job or career.
8. Write a letter to yourself. What three pieces of advice would you give yourself?
9. If you could change one thing about the world, what would it be?
10. Think about the most difficult problem you recently had. How did you handle it?
11. Write about five things you're passionate about. Do they have anything in common?
12. Write about a time when you felt most alive.
13. Describe your ideal apartment or house. What does it look like?
14. How do you typically deal with stress and anxiety?
15. Write about the best relationship you've experienced. It doesn't have to be romantic.
16. Describe your perfect date night or weekend getaway.
17. What talent do you wish you had? Why?
18. What do you wish you had more time for?

19. Have you achieved anything recently that you're proud of? Write about it.

20. If you could have a superpower, what would it be, and how would you use it?

Forget about finding the right answers and focus on being honest with yourself. Don't censor yourself; this isn't Instagram. Be raw, real, and unapologetic. It's how you figure out who you are and what you're here to do.

Meditation

Meditation is another way to connect with your soul and reveal your purpose. Everyone meditates differently. Some prefer to sit quietly, cross-legged, eyes closed, and focus intently on their breath. Some meditate better when they can move their bodies, like in walking meditation or light yoga. Others weave a little meditation into their regular activities, like doing laundry mindfully. Some people don't like to meditate. Who can blame them? Sitting like a yogi for hours doesn't sound like something anyone who isn't a yogi would want to do.

Thankfully, you're not a yogi, and you don't have to meditate like one to reap the benefits of this ancient practice. Meditation has evolved because people have evolved, but the end game is the same: to know yourself and to find inner peace. There is a guided meditation exercise below. However, you can meditate as you like. Every meditation has three markers that are adaptable to any preference. They are:

- **The Starting Point:** This is the part of your session where you get comfortable, preferably somewhere quiet. It could mean sitting down, lying down, going for a walk, starting your chores, etc. As long as it is a beginning that feels natural, not forced, it'll work. This is where you consciously decide to step away from the outside world and go inward.

- **The Journey:** This is the meat of the practice, where you focus on whatever you want, as long as it is repetitive. You can focus on your breath, an affirmation, or your body's sensations. Your mind is likely to wander; it happens to everyone. Gently guide your attention back to what it was focused on initially. It gets easier the more you practice.

- **The Landing:** You're at the end of your session, where you rejoin the world. You can take a few deep breaths, take a shower, eat, go out for some fresh air, or do whatever you need to integrate the peace and clarity from the concluded session.

If your session hit all three stages, congratulations, you just meditated. It doesn't matter if it was for five minutes, 10, or 30 – you meditated. Here is a guided meditation session for finding your purpose:

1. Get a comfortable seat. It can be on the floor, or if you prefer to lie down, go ahead. Allow your body to settle, and gently close your eyes. Set the intention of finding your soul's purpose. Know that this is the session's purpose.

2. Breathe in deeply once, twice, three times. With each exhale, release tension and distractions.

3. Imagine standing in a beautiful forest. The sunlight is filtering through the trees, the leaves are brilliantly green, a soft moss is beneath your feet, and you hear insects buzzing.

4. This forest represents your soul. Feel how peaceful it is. There is much wisdom in this place.

5. Begin walking through this forest. Take your time, look around, smell the air.

6. Keep an eye out for thoughts, images, or feelings that come to you. Don't force anything; trust your soul and let it lead the way.

7. Walk toward an ancient tree in the middle of this forest. It's up to you how far or how close this tree is. This tree represents the wisdom and guidance of your higher self. It knows your true purpose. Do you trust this tree? Do you feel safe around it?

8. When you feel safe, sit at the base of the tree and converse with it. What questions do you have about your life's purpose? What is the tree telling you?

9. Listen closely and freely. Don't try to manipulate the answers to fit what you want to hear. Know that the answers you seek are already within you.

10. When you're ready, slowly make your way out of the forest.

11. Take a few deep breaths and open your eyes.

Surrender to the Unknown

By now, you must know that everywhere you look, there is some advice on how to *"find your life purpose."*

You could say the same thing is happening right here, right now. Everyone is exchanging elaborate methods, long checklists, and step-by-step formulas to help you find your calling. Undoubtedly, these approaches are helpful for some. However, many are still lost, even after doing everything. What about doing nothing? How about a different process – one that's more about letting go than trying to control? Why force the issue and relentlessly pursue a predetermined idea of what your purpose should be when the wisest path may be to surrender to the mystery? You keep stressing and strategizing, but what if you just let go instead?

Surrendering and going with the flow might feel counterintuitive, especially if you're used to being in the driver's seat. Everyone has achieved something or is working hard toward achieving something, so the thought of loosening your grip and trusting the process could seem irresponsible. As scary as it is, you need to permit yourself to slow down and see what life is presenting you. What if you allowed yourself to be surprised, to follow unexpected breadcrumbs, and to say yes to things you never would have predicted?

Stop hunting down your purpose and let it find you. No, this doesn't translate to sitting back and doing nothing. There's still action required on your part, although the action looks a little different. This time, you must stay present and committed without attachment to an outcome. Trust that the answers will reveal themselves in due time. Don't see it as doing *"nothing."* You're choosing receptivity over-reactivity, and sometimes, that's all your soul needs from you. When the answers and opportunities come, and they will, you'll know what to do.

Chapter 3: Numerology and the Soul: Decoding Your Life Path

The entire universe is a giant mathematical formula. Everything that exists can be reduced to a mathematical formula inside a mathematical formula.

At the most fundamental level, the building blocks of all life – subatomic particles, forces, and fields – are governed by the rules of mathematics, and it doesn't stop at the smallest scales. The movement of planets, stars, and galaxies obeys the principles of mathematics according to classical mechanics and general relativity. Phenomena such as planetary orbits around the sun, the expansion of the universe, the propagation of light, and the atoms forming the cells in your body can be predicted and explained using mathematical formulas.

Numerology is a great tool to help decode your path.'

This undeniable connection between mathematics and reality gave birth to numerology, the study of the mystical and symbolic relationship between numbers and the physical world. Numerologists believe that everything can be reduced to a single-digit number, from 1 to 9. These numbers have powers and properties influencing people's lives, personalities, and experiences.

The History of Numerology

Numerology is popular today thanks to one man, Pythagoras. Pythagoras was a philosopher living in ancient Greece. Although he was born and raised there, he wasn't quite as Greek as history books would have you believe. His father was a Phoenician, and the Phoenicians were famous throughout the ancient world for seafaring and extensive trading networks. This Phoenician connection is in part responsible for how Pythagoras grew up because, as intelligent as he was, knowledge was very scarce in his time.

As the son of a wealthy Phoenician merchant, he had access to rooms, information, and people that were unheard of for the average ancient philosopher. Through his father's contacts and trading relationships, Pythagoras could study under the greatest minds in the ancient world, including Thales of Miletus, a few Egyptian high priests, Babylonian rabbis, and Themistoclea, a Delphi oracle. He rubbed elbows with Persian magicians, Phoenician kings, and Chaldeans, who were great thinkers and sages. These great minds were a long way from home for Pythagoras. Hence, it was this broad, cross-cultural education that led to his revolutionary ideas about numbers.

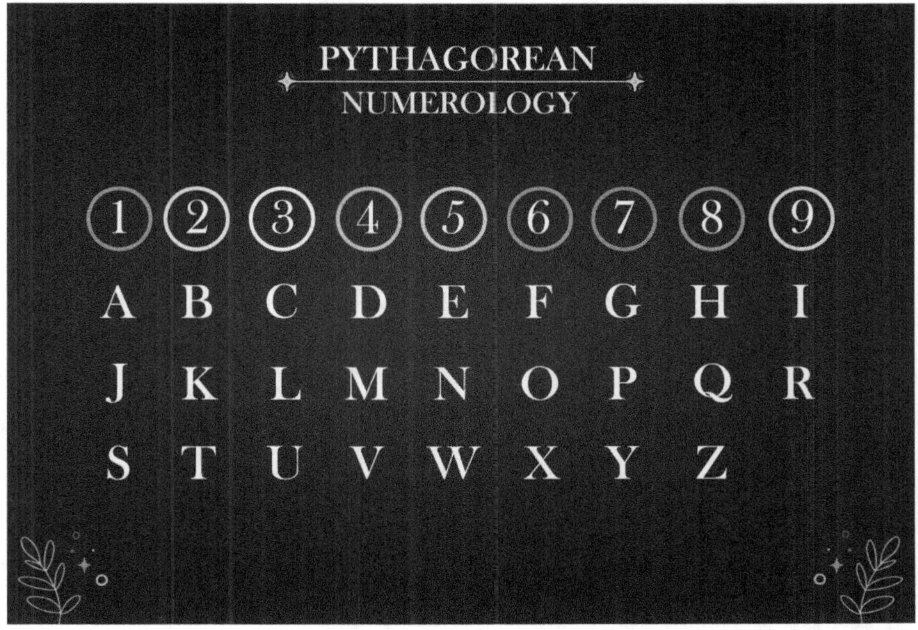

Pythagoras was convinced that there was a divine, numerical code embedded in all creation, and it was his mission to crack it. He started a school with this in mind, and the numerical implications of your name determined if you were admitted or not. Too far? Maybe, maybe not. Pythagoras wasn't the only one who believed that numbers could predict everything, even personalities. The Chaldeans were already doing this long before Pythagoras was born.

Chaldean Numerology

The Chaldeans were an ancient Mesopotamian people in Babylon, modern-day Iraq. Over 4000 years ago, they developed a system that assigned numerical values to their alphabet letters based on their position and frequency within the language. They believed that using these numerical values could predict a person's personality, talents, and destiny using only their name. Back then, people used nicknames, while their legal names remained a closely guarded secret to protect their destiny. Only mothers knew their children's real names.

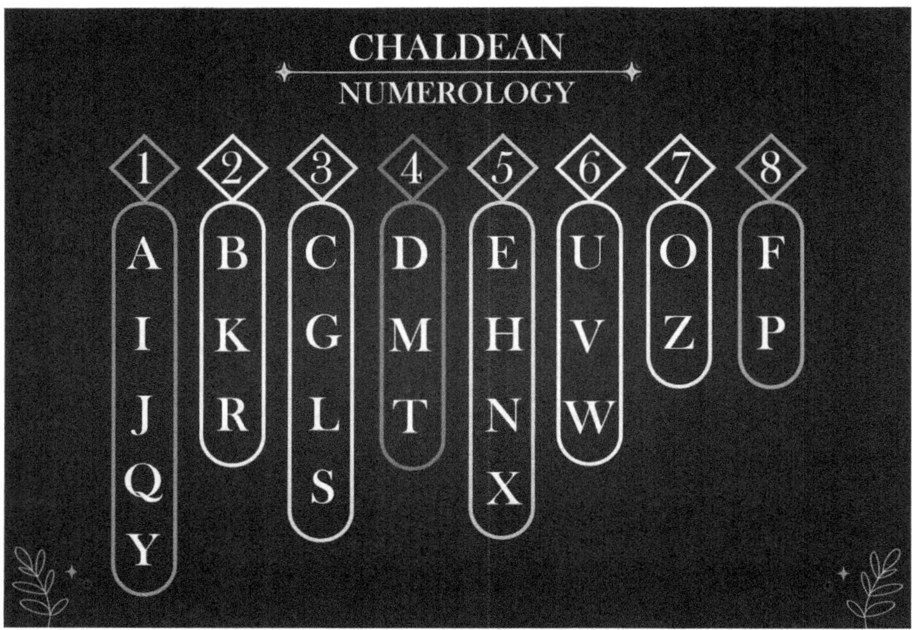

This numerology system became available to the Greeks after Alexander the Great invaded and conquered Babylon. If not for Chaldean numerology, the Pythagorean system never would've existed. Chaldeans believed that everything in the universe vibrates – produces invisible ripples or waves – and, like instruments, everything has a signature vibration. They understood that synchronized vibrations attract each other, and likewise, unbalanced vibrations attract the same.

Another interesting Chaldean belief is the predestination of life. They believed, without a doubt, that every life is a pre-written script and its destiny is set in stone, waiting to play out.

Sounds a lot like soul contracts. But 4,000 years ago? The Chaldeans thought that the numbers associated with the letters in your legal name and the numbers in your full birth date reveal your vibrational signature. This signature determines your life's course, your personality, your talents, and your destiny's defining milestones. Try as you might, you can't change the plot – your destiny is locked in from the minute you're born. You can see why it made sense to keep your birth name a secret in those days.

The Chaldeans figured out that you could tweak your script a little by changing your legal name. Destiny doesn't seem so locked in now, does it? According to this ancient civilization, if you officially change the letters of your identity, you could potentially alter its vibrational frequencies and partially rewrite said destiny. They were onto something because, to date, the Chaldean system is more precise and reliable than most forms of numerology.

Numerology and Other Mystical Traditions

Apart from Chaldean numerology, one of the oldest and most influential numerology traditions comes from the Jewish Kabbalah. Kabbalists were obsessed with the divinity in numbers, especially the first 10 numbers, which they believed to be divine emanations that created the universe.

Each of these 10 numbers, called the Sephirot, had a personality and meaning. For example, the number 1 symbolizes unity and new beginnings. The number 3 represents the balance between mind, body, and spirit. Number 7 represents perfection and spirituality. One of the earliest Kabbalistic works, the Sefer Yetzirah, explains the symbolic meanings of the first 10 numbers and how they relate to the 22 letters of the Hebrew

The Sephirot.[10]

alphabet. For these mystics, numbers weren't just neutral – they were portals straight to the divine. This practice is called *Gematria*.

The Jews weren't the only ones with something mystical to say about numbers. Numerology has been essential in Eastern cultures for centuries. The Chinese associate the numbers 1 through 9 with elements, directions, and philosophical principles. The number 8 is a lucky Chinese number because its Chinese name, *"ba"* rhymes with *"fa,"* which means good fortune. This is not secret knowledge; the 2008 Beijing Olympics opening ceremony took place at 8:08 pm on 8/8/08. Meanwhile, the number 4 is treated like the plague because they believe it represents bad luck and death.

Ancient Egyptians were interested in numbers. They were into a lot of things, but numerology was as important to them as it was to other corners of the world. It can only mean one thing: numbers are as important as they are mysterious; *be the missing piece to understanding your soul's purpose.*

Spiritual Meaning of Numbers

- **Number 1: The Leader**

  Number 1 centers around new beginnings, individuality, and taking the lead. It represents the pioneering spirit, innovation, and the need to blaze your own trail. Spiritually, the number 1 means self-reliance, confidence, and manifestation. It's a reminder to trust your intuition and fearlessly go against the grain.

- **Number 2: The Peacemaker**

  The number 2 embodies harmony, balance, and cooperation. It's the number of diplomacy, partnerships, and fairness. Spiritually, 2 represents the yin and yang, the divine feminine, and unity. If you see the number 2, you are being encouraged to be open-minded and empathetic and to work with others for the greater good.

- **Number 3: The Visionary**

  Number 3 symbolizes creativity, self-expression, and the mind. It's the number of the artist, the dreamer, and the visionary. Spiritually, 3 stands for the divine trinity, the life-giving force of the universe, and manifestation. Seeing this number should inspire you to communicate your truth, imagine more, and share your talents with the world.

- ### Number 4: The Builder

  The number 4 is structure, stability, and the practical application of ideas. It represents the builder and the organizer and brings order to chaos. Spiritually, 4 means protection, the four elements, and the need for discipline and diligence in everything you do.

- ### Number 5: The Adventurer

  Number 5 represents adventure, freedom, and a thirst for something new. It is for the explorer, the seeker, and those who embody change. Spiritually, it is used to represent the five senses and divine grace. It's a reminder to step out of your comfort zone, surrender to the unknown, and live life to the fullest.

- ### Number 6: The Caretaker

  This is the number of the caretaker and the healer who brings balance and healing. Spiritually, 6 represents the divine feminine, unconditional love, and the responsibility to care for others and the planet. It is compassion and safety for yourself and others.

- ### Number 7: The Seeker

  Number 7 is known worldwide for perfection. It is the number of spirituality, introspection, and the search for purpose. It is for the mystic, the philosopher, and the mysteries of the universe. Spiritually, it represents divine wisdom, intuition, and human connection with the unseen. It's a number that inspires you to go within, to question your beliefs, and to seek the truth that exists past the physical world's veil.

- ### Number 8: The Manifester

  Number 8 signifies abundance, power, and manifestation. It's for the entrepreneur, the leader, and those who have mastered the material world. It represents the infinity symbol, divine balance, and the mastery of the spiritual and earthly domains. This number encourages you to step into your power, use your resources wisely, and create a legacy.

- ### Number 9: The Humanitarian

  Number 9 symbolizes universal love and the desire to serve humanity. It's for the humanitarian, the visionary, and those who see the big picture. Spiritually, 9 represents divine completion, spiritual maturity, and transcendence. It's the number for altruism and a reminder to leave the world a better place than you found it.

Karmic Numerology

Karmic numerology is not very popular because karma has a reputation for being "bad," and people would rather not pour their energy into negativity. However, karma is not inherently bad. It doesn't mean you are a bad person. It means you have a few lessons to learn and karmic debts or unresolved issues from past lives that are carried over and manifested in your current life.

Your karmic number is only there to help you identify the unhealthy cycles and areas you agreed to work through in this lifetime so that they don't follow you into your next life. Karma is heavy, but the lessons are necessary, and the quicker you drop the baggage, the faster you can move on, light as a feather.

In karmic numerology, the two main branches are karmic lesson numbers and karmic debt numbers.

Karmic Lesson Numbers

Your karmic lesson number is any number that is missing from the numerology of your full legal name. The missing numbers represent a skill or trait that is lacking or weak, a void you must fill. For example, suppose your name is Smith Darius Wilson. In that case, your numerology will be *1 4 9 2 8 4 1 9 9 3 1 5 9 3 1 6 5*, starting from the first letter in your first name to the last letter in your last name. Looking at these numbers, only one number is missing, number 7. So, your karmic lesson number is 7. Some people don't have karmic lesson numbers, but that doesn't mean they don't have karma. Remember the other branch of karmic numerology: karmic debt number.

For those with karmic lesson numbers, here are your karmic lessons for this lifetime:

- **Number 1:**

  If you're missing the number 1, you could have problems taking charge and decision-making. You might wait for people to tell you what to do instead of taking the initiative. Your life lesson is to become more self-motivated and confident. You'll need to stand up to strong-willed people who try to control you and stop procrastinating.

- **Number 2:**

With a missing 2, you need to work on being more cooperative and considerate. You may prefer to stay in the background instead of putting yourself out there. Your lesson is to learn diplomacy, patience, and how to be a team player. Consideration of how your actions affect those around you will help you build stronger relationships.

- **Number 3:**

If your karmic lesson number is 3, you may be extremely self-critical. You might struggle with imposter syndrome or think you've done a terrible job even when others are impressed. Your lesson is to accept that no one is perfect and become more optimistic. Be proud of whatever you do, even if it isn't flawless.

- **Number 4:**

Without a 4, you could feel lost and uncertain of the right life path to take. You must work on being more organized, disciplined, and grounded. Finding the right job or career might be tricky, but when you find it, stick with it and put in the hard work because it will pay off.

- **Number 5:**

For a karmic lesson 5, your lesson is to become more adventurous and adaptable. You probably don't like to try new things or step out of your comfort zone. You need to stay receptive to change, take risks, and have faith that you can handle whatever life throws at you.

- **Number 6:**

A karmic lesson 6 has commitment issues. You may run away or keep people at arm's length because it feels safer. Your lesson is to learn how to build and sustain serious, genuine relationships. You must learn vulnerability.

- **Number 7:**

For a karmic lesson 7, you must develop your talents and reach mastery at whatever you do. You might prefer only to skim the surface of things. Your lesson is to put in the time and effort to master a skill or subject that speaks to you.

- **Number 8:**

  A missing 8 has the potential to be financially successful, but you may not be very good at managing your money. Your lesson is to learn your limits and find balance. Don't take on too much risk, or you could have trouble holding onto your wealth.

- **Number 9:**

  You need a lesson in compassion. You need to find ways to stay connected to the world around you. Sometimes, you must take the spotlight off yourself and consider the greater good. Think of the bigger picture and make sacrifices for your community.

Karmic Debt Number

The choices you make and how you live have consequences that carry over from one life to the next. Your karmic debt number represents the vibrational energies of these consequences. It is calculated using your full birth date. Unlike the karmic lesson number, this number is derived from the numbers that are present.

Karmic debt numbers are from 13 to 19. So, if your full birth date adds up to any of these numbers, you have a karmic debt number. Each number's meaning is:

- **Number 13:** If you have a 13 karmic debt, you're someone who puts a lot of effort into everything you do. You're a hard worker, but sometimes, you may not like this about yourself because it feels like there's always something in your way, no matter how hard you try. You might have felt tempted to give up many times. Ironically, many successful people have a 13 karmic debt, but they made it because they kept going and remained focused. Focus doesn't come easy to karmic debt 13s. Their attention is almost always spread out across too many projects. They jump from one thing to the next and never give anything their full effort. It's where they run into trouble. If this is you, you need to pick a goal and stick to it. Forget about taking shortcuts. The easy way out hardly ever works for 13s. Stay organized, keep to a schedule, and follow through on what you start. That's your lesson.

- **Number 14:** Karmic debt 14s misused their freedom in the past. Now, they're being forced to adapt to unexpected changes and random occurrences. They're at risk of turning to unhealthy coping mechanisms like drugs, alcohol, or overindulgence, so another life lesson is moderation. If you're a karmic debt 14, you have no choice but to be flexible and adaptable. Life has thrown you too many curveballs already, and it doesn't look like it's slowing down. You will need to take life as it comes, but still keep your eye on your goals. If you want something, you need to want it badly enough to stay committed even when you're repeatedly redirected. Keep your goals high and your indulgences low. Above all, don't give up on your dreams. It's okay to be afraid, but trust that the redirections are taking you where you want to go. Don't take your eye off the prize, and don't give up.

- **Number 16:** This karmic debt is transformation and renewal. The old self must be torn down to make way for the new. Karmic debt 16s are deep thinkers and highly intuitive people. They have the potential for great spiritual growth but run the risk of egoism and looking down on others. They are prone to alienation and loneliness. The 16 teaches you to let go of the structures and beliefs that have kept you separate from your true self and higher consciousness. It might be a painful process, watching the collapse of the life you've built, but on the other side of the destruction is a rebirth. With the 16, life will keep presenting you with choices and situations that force you to let go of your grand plans and ambitions. It's frustrating, but it's part of the process. Be humble and trust your intuition, but also be practical in how you apply your wisdom.

- **Number 19:** Karmic debt 19 teaches you about hyperindependence and the responsible use of power. You may experience many situations where you're forced to stand up for yourself and go it alone. One of your main lessons in this lifetime is to work through your stubborn resistance to accepting help. You want to be self-sufficient so badly that you forget everyone and everything is connected and interdependent, no matter how much you might want to be an island unto yourself. You must find the right balance between independence and connection. You need to learn that it's okay to rely on someone else and receive help. You don't have to do everything on your own.

You're a risk taker, and there's a saying among risk takers, "If you want something done well, do it yourself." This is true, except that even the most independent and capable people need help sometimes. Ask for help; otherwise, your independence quickly becomes a prison.

Master Numbers

Master numbers are special life path numbers. They are different, not because they are identical double digits but because of the digits. Master numbers are 11, 22, and 33 because of the numbers 1, 2, and 3. Other identical double digits – 55, 88, 44 – are also special. However, they are power numbers, not master numbers, and not life path numbers.

People with master numbers are extraordinary, but with great power comes great responsibility. Here's what this means:

- **11:**

    Master number 11s are the messengers or the illuminators. This number has been tied to intuition, idealism, and spiritual enlightenment. Generally, anyone with 11 as a master number is extremely sensitive, empathetic, and plugged into the spirit world. Their heightened awareness connects them to higher planes of consciousness. They are natural healers, teachers, and visionaries who inspire and assist others. The 11s are known for their creativity, imagination, and appetite for knowledge, but they also carry a heavy burden. The increased sensitivity of this number makes them prone to anxiety, overthinking, and feeling almost drowned in the world's energy. They may have a hard time with self-doubt, insecurity, and perfectionism. Despite their mastery, the 11s must learn to balance the spiritual and the practical – and the intuitive and the logical. They must learn to manage their sensitivity and find practical applications for their gifts or risk being swallowed by them. They might be conduits of light and wisdom, but they need stability and balance in the physical world.

- **22:**

    Master number 22, typically called the "master builder" or the "master manifesto," is the most powerful of the three master numbers. It is known for ambition, leadership, and big dreams. People with 22 as a master number are natural problem-solvers and strategists. They have an eye for detail and the foresight to plan for the long term. The 22s are practical and organized. They take an idea and transform it into something tangible. They don't believe in limitations; if they don't have the resources, they'll find them. This is a blessing and a curse because the 22s also suffocate under the pressure of their potential. The high expectations they set for themselves and the world cause burnout, stress, and inadequacy. It's never enough for a 22, but they need to learn that, sometimes, it is. Some 22s are controlling or obsessive in their quest for perfection. There is a balance between ambition and compassion, and every 22 needs to find it. They must learn to delegate, trust others, and make time for self-care.

- **33:**

   The 33s are the master teachers and healers. This number is associated with unconditional love, universal wisdom, and commitment to service. The 33s feel a chronic desire to help people and make the world a better place. They are the teachers, counselors, and guides, which explains their extraordinary patience, empathy, and understanding of the human experience. However, the weight of their responsibilities can quickly become too much for them to handle. They may experience burnout, not be very good at setting boundaries, and will almost always overextend themselves. The 33s must learn to balance their need to serve with the need to honor themselves. Their love and selfless service must be grounded in wisdom because no one can pour from an empty cup.

Core Numbers in Numerology

Life Path Number

Your life path number is the most important part of your numerology report. It reveals your life journey and purpose. To figure out your life path number, add the digits in your birth date, then reduce that sum to a single digit.

For example, if you were born on March 15, 1985, your calculation would be:

3 *(for March)* + 15 *(for the day)* + 1 + 9 + 8 + 5 *(for the year)* = 41

4 + 1 = 5

So, someone born on March 15, 1985, would have a life path number of 5.

Each life path number, from 1 to 9, has identifiable themes and characteristics.

- **Life path 1s** are natural leaders. They are confident, decisive, and unafraid to take charge.

- **Life path 2s** are diplomatic and sensitive. They value peace, empathy, and cooperation.

- **Life path 3s** are creative and expressive. They are charismatic, friendly, and optimistic. They enjoy entertaining or inspiring people.

- **Life path 4s** are practical, detail-oriented, and hardworking. They like structure, organization, and getting things done the right way.

- **Life path 5s** are adventurous and adaptable. They love new experiences, freedom, and variety. The 5s get bored with routine and are always eager to try the next new thing. They are curious, spontaneous, and open-minded.

- **Life path 6s** are nurturing and responsible. They want nothing more than to care for people and make a positive difference in the world.

- **Life path 7s** are introspective and analytical. They like to know things. The 7s are private, contemplative, and drawn to spiritual or intellectual activities.

- **Life path 8s** are extremely goal-oriented. If they understand anything, it's business, leadership, and material success. The 8s are ambitious, disciplined, and bold.

- **Life path 9s** are compassionate, empathetic, and idealistic. Like 6s, they want to make the world a better place and might prefer creative, artistic, or service-oriented roles.

Expression Number

This core number is calculated using your full birth name (first, middle, and last) and represents your natural talents, skills, and potential. To know your expression number, you take the numerical value of each letter in each name, add them, reduce the numbers per name to a single digit, and then reduce that to a single digit.

Using the name Harvey Reginald Specter as an example, the calculation would be:

H(8) + **A**(1) + **R**(9) + **V**(4) + **E**(5) + **Y**(7) = 34.

3+4=7

R(9) + **E**(5) + **G**(7) + **I**(9) + **N**(5) + **A**(1) + **L**(3) + **D**(4) = 43

4+3=7

S(1) + **P**(7) + **E**(5) + **C**(3) + **T**(2) + **E**(5) + **R**(9) = 32

3+2 = 5

7+7+5=19

1+9=10

1+0=1

So, the expression number for Harvey Reginald Specter would be 1. Here's what each expression number means:

- **Number 1:** Number 1s are very independent and confident. You're not afraid to take risks and try new things. You prefer the freedom to make your own decisions.

- **Number 2:** Number 2s are more intuitive and sensitive than most. You seek out balance, and you'd rather resolve conflicts peacefully. You're good at working with others, but you get thrown off by negativity.

- **Number 3:** You're outgoing and optimistic, with a creative, uplifting energy. People find you inspiring. You're drawn to the arts or other expressive outlets, but don't let yourself become too cynical, irresponsible, or undisciplined.

- **Number 4:** Number 4s are practical, methodical, and grounded. You're a reliable and responsible person. You come off as very stable with family and at work. You're also very stubborn.

- **Number 5:** With a number 5, you likely love freedom, excitement, and everything new. You're an adaptable free spirit who makes it a point to avoid routines and social norms. You also change your mind too often, get bored too quickly, or leave things unfinished.

- **Number 6:** 6s are loving and honest. In any circle, you're always the healer or counselor. You are the most likely to sacrifice your time and energy to care for the people around you. To some people, this comes off as too overprotective or an inability to stay out of other people's business.

- **Number 7:** 7s are as inquisitive as they are intelligent. Always on the hunt for truth, knowledge, and wisdom, you're more introverted and prefer having your own space and alone time to work on your projects. People might complain that you're secretive or disconnected.

- **Number 8:** Expression number 8s are ambitious, disciplined, and hardworking. These qualities, along with your planning skills, attention to detail, and realistic foresight, always lead you to great success.

- **Number 9:** Number 9s are interested in anything that promises to make the world a better place. You're idealistic, humanitarian, and a visionary. Don't let yourself be taken advantage of.

Personality Number

Your personality number is the filter through which the world sees you, at least at first. It's the impression people get when they first meet you or if your interactions are surface-level. Your personality number influences the energy and characteristics you put out there. It determines the people and information you're drawn to and the information you're comfortable putting out into the world.

Your personality number is calculated with the numerical value of the consonants in your full name.

So, Harry James Potter's personality number is:

H(8) + **R**(9) + **R**(9)= 26

2+6= 8

J(1) + **M**(4) + **S**(1)= 6

P(7) + **T**(2) + **T**(2) + **R**(9)= 20

2+0= 2

8+6+2= 16

1+6= 7

Harry's personality number is 7, and each personality number has a distinct meaning.

- **Number 1:**

You come across as ambitious and confident. People see you as someone who knows what they want. Still, you need to be careful not to seem too egotistical or intimidating.

- **Number 2:**

You have a friendly and trustworthy energy. People are attracted to your warmth and approachability. You're the one they come to for help, but you must watch for indecisiveness or being seen as a pushover.

- **Number 3:**

You are charming and creative. Your wit and optimism are your most attractive qualities, but you must be cautious that you don't come off as superficial or exaggerated.

- **Number 4:**

People see you as reliable, organized, and great at getting things done. They trust your judgment and knowledge, especially in business. However, try not to be too serious or predictable.

- **Number 5:**

You have a daring and passionate spirit. People find you inspiring, but some might think you're too aloof or superficial.

- **Number 6:**

Your personality is warm and caring. You're everyone's go-to for emotional support. As agreeable as you are, you need to ensure you're not being taken advantage of.

- **Number 7:**

Your aura is more reserved and intellectual. People respect your intelligence but find it hard to get to know the real you. Try not to appear too opinionated or arrogant.

- **Number 8:**

You project a strong, ambitious, and confident energy. You are a capable leader and good decision-maker. However, some might think you are egocentric or greedy.

- **Number 9:**

  Your charisma is your selling point. People love your idealism and positivity, but there's a risk of seeming too arrogant or above others.

Soul Urge Number

The final core number is the soul urge number, called the heart's desire number. This number reveals your heart's desires and motivations. To calculate the soul urge number, you take only the vowels in your full birth name (including Y if it produces a vowel sound when the name is pronounced) and add their numerical values.

Using Harry James Potter as an example again, the calculation would be:

A(1) + **Y**(7)= 8

A(1) + **E**(5)= 6

O(6) + **E**(5)= 11

8+6+11= 25

2+5=7

The soul urge number for Harry James Potter is 7.

Here are the meanings of soul urge numbers from 1 to 9:

- **Number 1:** Soul urge number 1s are independent and motivated to be in charge.

- **Number 2:** Number 2s want harmony, peace, and security.

- **Number 3:** 3s are creative, imaginative, and sociable.

- **Number 4:** 4s find comfort in routine, structure, organization, and stability.

- **Number 5:** Number 5s long for freedom, variety, and new experiences.

- **Number 6:** 6s are motivated by compassion, empathy, and sacrifice.

- **Number 7:** 7s are introspective and introverted.

- **Number 8:** 8s want authority and influence.

- **Number 9:** 9s are idealistic and philanthropic.

Applications of Numerology

- **Making Decisions**

  Numerology can help with decision-making. For example, deciding between two job offers. Say one is with a company that has the expression number 7, and the other is a company with the expression number 3. Suppose 7 fits better with your numerological profile. In that case, there's a good possibility that the role and work culture is a better fit for your strengths and tendencies. The number 3 company may be too social and extroverted unless that's what you're looking for. This numerological information could help you make the best choice for your success.

- **Choosing Dates**

  Your wedding date is an important decision. You want to pick a day that will bring good luck and usher you into a happy marriage. You can choose the best date by calculating the numeric value of potential wedding dates. This will tell you what days of the month have the most favorable numerological qualities for your wedding or other events.

- **Understanding Your Relationships**

  The dating scene is chaotic. If you want an idea of your romantic compatibility from the start, you can calculate the numeric values of both your names. You may learn that while your profiles have some good synergies, the numeric relationship between you has a hidden 8 energy, which could mean power struggles and control issues. Now, you can have a healthy conversation with your person about setting healthy boundaries and communication patterns to nip this potential friction in the bud.

- **Timing Is Everything**

  Mostly, it's not how you do a thing – but when. Assuming you're preparing to ask your boss for a raise, you can check the numeric value of the upcoming week to know what energies will be at play. Then, you can strategically schedule your meeting for the best day, knowing that the numerological influences will be working in your favor. This timing could give you an extra edge and increase your chances of getting what you want.

Chapter 4: Astrology and the Soul Plan: How the Stars Align with Your Divine Purpose

Looking up at the sky, you could think you're a small, insignificant speck compared to over 100 billion galaxies and even more stars that fill the sky. However, astrology is evidence that the universe is anything but impersonal. Astrologers believe that the positions and movements of planets, stars, and constellations are more influential on human affairs than we think. They're not wrong. There is order beneath the apparent chaos, even if nobody fully understands it. Scientists might disagree; they see the universe as a large, mechanical system governed by the laws of physics. They're not wrong, either. The universe is so unimaginably massive that humanity may never understand. Astrology is a 5000-year-old system that hasn't failed yet. Something about it defies skepticism. If not, horoscopes would've gone extinct, and nobody would care about their natal chart.

The stars are relevant to your soul purpose.[11]

Skepticism aside, nothing is still, even according to science. Stasis doesn't exist. Everything is always spinning and interacting with everything else. Your body, objects, plants, animals, and the ground beneath your feet might look stationary, but they're not. Since there is movement on Earth, so is there movement in the sky, with the planets, stars, and other celestial bodies perpetually orbiting and shifting. The macrocosm and microcosm are so interconnected that what happens in the stars above customarily reflects on the earth below, and your natal chart is this interconnectedness made manifest. It is a concrete and detectable proof of movement in the heavens. Your natal chart shows you precisely where every celestial body was when you were born. Each position carries an energetic imprint replicated in the different facets of your life.

Components of the Natal Chart

Sun Signs

When interpreting and understanding a natal chart, the sun sign is treated as the most important and defining aspect of the entire chart. Your sun sign, which is determined by the sun's position at your birth, is the essence of your astrological personality.

Astrologically, it determines your identity and how you choose to express yourself externally. It represents your ego, your will, your intensity, and your purpose. So, what does your sun sign say about you?

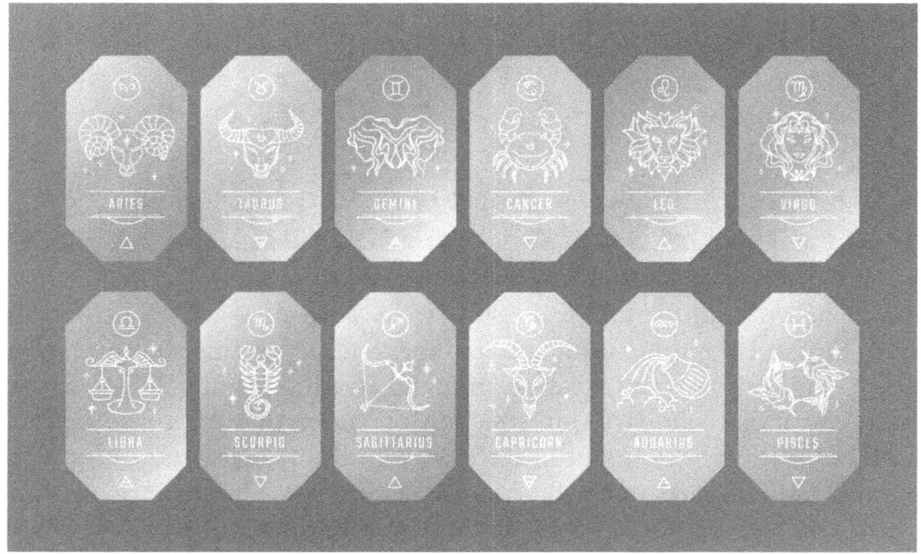

The sun signs.[12]

- **Aries (March 21 - April 19)**

  Being the first sign of the zodiac, Aries people are born pioneers – adventurous, courageous, and always eager to make a way for themselves. They have an independent spirit and a need to be first, to be the best, and to lead the charge. Aries suns are impulsive, energetic, and confident. They are not afraid to take risks and meet their problems head-on. Unfortunately, they can also be impatient, hot-headed, and quick to anger if they don't get their way.

- **Taurus (April 20 - May 20)**

  Taurus sun signs are known for their stability, practicality, and love for creature comforts. They are sensual, down-to-earth people who find joy in life's simple pleasures – good food, art, and comfortable surroundings. They're quite hardheaded, though, and dislike change the minute it interferes with their routine. They can be indulgent, possessive, and resistant to leaving their comfort zones.

- **Gemini (May 21 - June 20)**

  Gemini suns are the social butterflies of the zodiac – curious, communicative, and forever adaptable. They have a youthful, versatile energy and an insatiable intellectual appetite. They're always ready to learn something new or have a stimulating conversation. Geminis are charming, quick-witted, and great multitaskers, but they can also be indecisive, scatterbrained, and two-faced.

- **Cancer (June 21 - July 22)**

  Cancer sun signs are nurturers and caretakers. They are intuitive, emotional, and security-oriented people who place a high value on family, home, and their closest relationships. Cancers have a strong maternal instinct and a propensity for being protective, sensitive, and sentimental. The downside is they can be moody and clingy and have difficulty letting go of the past.

- **Leo (July 23 - August 22)**

  Leo sun signs were born to be performers and leaders. They are regal, confident, and have a flair for the dramatic. They want all the spotlight and admiration but are quite generous and charismatic. If you have a problem with a Leo, it's likely because you've seen them be arrogant, demanding, and easily offended if they don't receive the attention and respect they feel they deserve.

- **Virgo (August 23 - September 22)**

  The methodical perfectionism of this sun sign is a blessing and a curse. They have a good eye for detail, a practical, analytical disposition, and a compelling need to do things for people. Virgos are hardworking, conscientious, and good at problem-solving. Still, they are too critical, fussy, and anxious when things aren't going according to plan.

- **Libra (September 23 - October 22)**

  Libra suns are diplomats and peacemakers. They are charming, graceful, and elegant people who will do almost anything for balance and justice. Libras are skilled negotiators, mediators, and social butterflies. However, they can be indecisive, people-pleasing, and avoidant.

- **Scorpio (October 23 - November 21)**

  There is no sign as intense, mysterious, and passionate as Scorpio. They have a magnetic, penetrating aura about them and are very curious about anything hidden or considered taboo. They are brave, loyal, and resourceful but can be possessive and vengeful, with many trust issues.

- **Sagittarius (November 22 - December 21)**

  Sagittarius suns are always where the fun is. They love a good time like nobody else. They have a boundless curiosity about the world, a philosophical, optimistic outlook, and always want to know more. They are jovial, honest, and energetic people but can be reckless, impatient, and noncommittal.

- **Capricorn (December 22 - January 19)**

  Capricorn suns are ambitious, disciplined, and pragmatic. Some would say they are the opposite of Sagittarius. They want nothing more than to achieve their goals and come off as mature and very responsible. A Capricorn is stable and will never let you down, but you may find them too serious, pessimistic, and unable to relax.

- **Aquarius (January 20 - February 18)**

  Aquarius sun signs are not hard to recognize. They are unconventional visionaries and intellectual rebels. They are progressive, humanitarian, and would love nothing more than to challenge the status quo. Aquarius suns are independent, objective, and usually ahead of their time, but they can be aloof, detached, and emotionally disconnected.

- **Pisces (February 19 - March 20)**

  It has been said that Pisces suns have a bit of all the zodiac signs in them. They are the mystics and the dreamers. Their sensitivity, intuition, and empathy are their best and worst qualities. Of all the zodiac signs, they have the strongest connection to the spirit world. Pisceans are imaginative and romantic but can be idealistic, escapist, and unable to set boundaries.

Moon Sign

The moon always comes second to the sun. It is quiet in the backseat, and happy to be there. Although it doesn't demand the spotlight, that does not mean it isn't equally important. In astrology, the sun represents your outward personality and the face everyone sees, but the moon is what you hide beneath. It represents your emotions, your subconscious, and your base instincts – the *you* the world doesn't get to see.

Your moon sign hints at how you process feelings, what you define as safe, and how you connect to your intuition. The closest people to you may get to see this side of you, but generally, it is private. It is the WHY behind the WHAT.

Here's what your moon sign says about you:

- **Aries moon:** People with an Aries moon have very active, energetic emotions. They feel things intensely and react quickly. Their moods change suddenly, and they aren't afraid to boldly express their feelings, even if it's impulsive. They wear their hearts on their sleeves.

- **Taurus moon:** Taurus moon people are emotionally steady and grounded. They want comfort, security, and pleasure. They're emotionally reliable and nurturing but stubborn and hate when things change too quickly.

- **Gemini moon:** Those with a Gemini moon have quite changeable, curious emotions. You could say their emotions are butterflies fluttering from one feeling to the next. Their moods and thoughts flow as quickly as their thoughts. They like variety and mental stimulation, so their emotions lean toward being scattered or indecisive.

- **Cancer moon:** Cancer moons are sensitive and intuitive. They're deeply in touch with their feelings and are always searching for emotional closeness and home. They can be moody and clingy – but just as caring and nurturing.

- **Leo moon:** Leo moons have big, dramatic emotions. They look for attention, admiration, and validation when expressing themselves. Their feelings are fiery and proud – and a tad self-centered.

- **Virgo moon:** Virgo moon types approach their emotions practically, analytically, and meticulously. They can be especially critical of themselves and others emotionally because they want everything to be perfect. They worry a lot and get entangled in small emotional issues, but they are more discerning than any other zodiac.

- **Libra moon:** Libra moons want peace, balance, and social connection in their emotional lives. As charming and people-pleasing as they are, they're somewhat indecisive about their feelings because they'd rather have consensus and validation from people.

- **Scorpio moon:** Scorpio moons have emotions that are as intense and scary as the dark depths of the ocean. They're intuitive, mysterious, and secretive. They brood a lot, too.

- **Sagittarius moon:** Sagittarius moons are as free-spirited as they come. Emotionally, they want expansion, optimism, and new experiences. They are direct, restless, and philosophically inclined with their feelings.

- **Capricorn moon:** Capricorn moons handle their emotions with discipline, responsibility, and practicality. Anyone can see that they are emotionally reserved, ambitious, and a little melancholic. Stability and structure are vital for them whenever emotions are involved.

- **Aquarius moon:** Aquarius moon types have a detached, independent emotional style. They prefer to observe rather than engage. Overt emotional expression doesn't come easily to these people, so they prefer to process feelings through the intellect. They are not sentimental and would rather do things for the greater good.

- **Pisces moon:** Pisces moons are empathetic and in touch with their subconscious. Their feelings can be fluid, compassionate, and maybe even psychic, but they might get lost in unrealistic daydreams from time to time.

Rising Sign

The rising sign, known as the Ascendant, is one of the most important elements in a person's birth chart. It is the star sign that was rising on the eastern horizon at birth. Your rising sign is a tint on your worldview and your initial response to your circumstances. It's the first impression you make on people and the energy you radiate. Unlike your Sun sign, which is your identity, your Ascendant is your external self – your style, mannerisms, and habits. It is how your soul has chosen to interface with the physical world in this lifetime. It's the portal through which your essence manifests in human form.

What is your rising sign?

- **Aries ascendant:** They have a strong competitive streak that appears without them realizing it. They may inadvertently take over conversations or push their agenda, not understanding why everyone else doesn't match their bold, impatient energy.

- **Taurus ascendant:** Taurus ascendants appreciate the finer things in life. They love to indulge their senses, which is good until they become too attached to their material possessions.

- **Gemini ascendant:** Geminis are too curious. It is hard work for them to focus on one thing for too long before moving on to the next shiny idea. Hence, they are versatile but also hyperactive and inattentive.

- **Cancer ascendant:** Cancer ascendants pick up on the unspoken feelings and energies of people, whether they want to or not. They smother the people they care about.

- **Leo ascendant:** Leos are outgoing and confident, but they can occasionally come off as arrogant or showmanship.

- **Virgo ascendant:** Perfectionists to their core, Virgos as ascendants can be critical of themselves and everyone around them. They may worry about minor details, especially when they have too many options.

- **Libra ascendant:** Libra ascendants hate conflict and will go to great lengths to avoid it, even if it means compromising their values or opinions.

- **Scorpio ascendant:** Scorpio ascendants are private. The people closest to them know this about them and have made their peace with it. Scorpios will hold a grudge or get revenge if they feel they've been wronged.

- **Sagittarius ascendant:** As freedom-loving as they are, they can be a bit tactless or insensitive when expressing their bold opinions. Relationships or long-term plans might make them feel trapped.

- **Capricorn ascendant:** Driven and ambitious, Capricorn ascendants might seem aloof or cold. They don't know how to let their guard down. Their professional and social image matters more than anything.

- **Aquarius ascendant:** Aquarius ascendants could seem detached or dispassionate. They're not. They would sooner rationalize their emotions than fully feel and express them.

- **Pisces ascendant:** They feel everything all the time as intensely as possible. They don't believe they need boundaries, but they do.

Planetary Placements

The sun and moon aren't the only celestial bodies in your birth chart. Everybody knows their sun and star sign, few people know their moon sign and even fewer people know their other planetary placements. Every celestial body in the solar system is always in a zodiac sign. Your birth chart shows the precise zodiac sign all the planets were in when you were born.

Not counting the sun and moon, they've already been covered. There are nine planets in the solar system, each with its own energies and characteristics. The positions of these planets at your birth weren't random; they were intentionally chosen and stipulated in your soul contract. You must first understand each planet's energy to understand why.

Each planet has its own energy.[18]

Mercury

Mercury, the closest planet to the sun, is the planet that rules communication, intellect, and how you process information. As the messenger of the gods in Greek mythology, this planet governs your daily routines, problem-solving skills, and even how funny you are. Your Mercury sign influences how you express yourself, verbally and in writing. People with multiple Mercury placements usually have a sharp wit, lively curiosity, and talent for anything logic and analysis.

Venus

This planet is in charge of relationships, self-worth, and appreciation for the finer things. Venus is the Roman version of the Greek goddess Aphrodite, who is the embodiment of love, beauty, and pleasure. A Venus placement influences your approach to romantic partnerships, what you find aesthetically pleasing, and, in part, your financial tendencies. For example, Venus in Libra. To them, diplomacy and compromise matter most in their relationships, while a Venus in Taurus might be more into sensual indulgences and material things. Your Venus sign could help you understand your love language – how you prefer to receive love.

Mars

Mars represents physical energy, your drive, and your capacity for action. With links to the Greek god of war, Ares, your Mars sign shows how you prefer to assert yourself, how you channel your sexual energy and the physical activities that strengthen you, not drain you. A strong Mars placement means intensity, a competitive spirit, and instinctive leadership. For example, a person with Mars in Cancer might enjoy workout routines with a mind-body connection, while a Mars in Gemini might prefer the variety and mental stimulation of high-intensity interval training.

Jupiter

Jupiter is the largest planet in the solar system – the planet of luck, growth, and expansion. It has ties to the Greek god Zeus, ruler of the sky, grandeur, and abundance. Your Jupiter sign can show you the areas where you have the highest chances of experiencing good fortune and personal growth. Multiple Jupiter placements come with a natural joie de vivre and a belief in possibility.

Saturn

Saturn is called the taskmaster. This planet rules over discipline, structure, and the lessons you must learn to grow and mature. Your Saturn sign shows you where you might run into problems and limitations and where you'll need hard work and persistence. Saturn placements are serious, responsible, and firmly committed to their goals. For example, a Saturn in Aries might be impulsive and need to learn patience. In contrast, a Saturn in Libra desperately needs balance and compromise in their relationships.

Uranus

Uranus is the go-to for innovation, eccentricity, and freedom because of its association with the Greek god Ouranos, the original ruler of the sky and the embodiment of rebellion. Your Uranus sign could point you to your talents and your readiness to defy the natural order. Multiple Uranus placements normally have a pioneering spirit. They love originality and nonconformity.

Neptune

Neptune is the planet linked to the subconscious, spirituality, and the blurred boundaries between reality and fantasy. It has links to the Greek god Poseidon, ruler of the seas, lending to its mystery and the unknown. Your Neptune placements determine your intuition, your creative inclinations, and your penchant for escapism. Strong Neptune placements are highly sensitive and fascinated with the metaphysical. Neptune in Pisces is considered a strong placement because Pisces is already ruled by Neptune. So, this person will feel a stronger connection to the mystical than a Neptune in Virgo.

Pluto

Pluto is the planet with the strongest links to the human experience. It is connected to the Greek god Hades, the god of the underworld. Your Pluto placements show the parts of your life that require the most personal growth, where you need to release old patterns and transform. People with strong Pluto placements have an intensity about them. They are passionate and willing to march into the darkest regions of their psyche if needed.

The Twelve Houses of Astrology

The 12 houses in astrology represent the different spheres or areas of human life. They follow the developmental journey your soul takes, from the initial spark that separates your identity (1st house) to the inevitable dissolution back into the collective (12th house). The houses are not "energies" like the zodiac or planets. They are the fields or domains where those energies are most likely expressed. The houses are the WHERE, and the planets and zodiac are the WHAT. Here's a quick tour through the 12 houses:

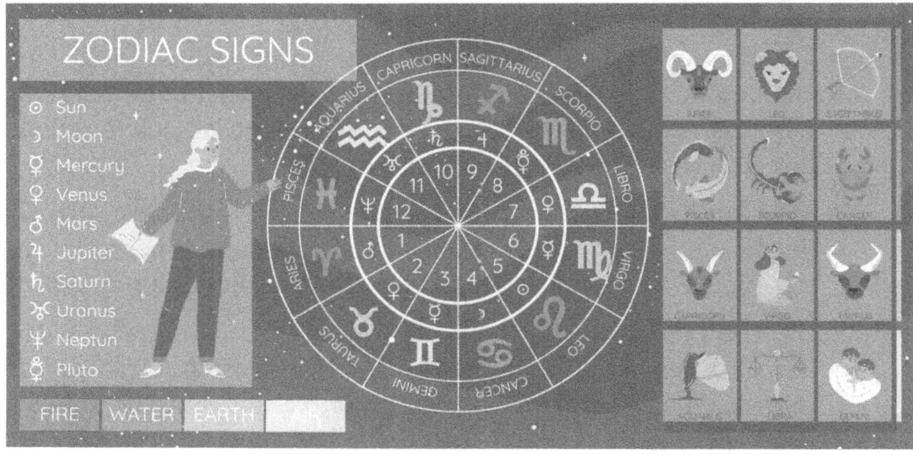

There are 12 houses in astrology.[14]

- **1st House:** This is the house of the self – your personality, physical appearance, self-image, and how you initiate action. Energies here have a strong influence on your identity and first impressions.

- **2nd House:** This house is in charge of your resources, values, and self-worth. It deals with your relationship to money, possessions, and your hidden talents. Energies here influence how you earn, save, and spend.

- **3rd House:** Communication, information, transportation, and your immediate environment are the domain of the 3rd house. It includes siblings, neighbors, short journeys, early education, and the workings of your lower, analytical mind.

- **4th House:** Home, family, foundations, and the emotional roots that anchor you are represented by the 4th house. Energies here influence your domestic life, parental relationships, and personal security.

- **5th House:** This is the house of self-expression, pleasure, and the heart. It rules romance, creativity, children, hobbies, and risk-taking. Energies here spark joy, fun, and authentic self-display.

- **6th House:** Daily work, routine, service, and physical health fall under the 6th house. Energies here influence your work ethic, habits, and how you manage mundane responsibilities.

- **7th House:** Partnerships, one-on-one relationships, love affairs, etc., come into focus in the 7th house, including marriage, business collaborations, and open enemies. Energies here affect how you relate and cooperate with people.

- **8th House:** The 8th house rules over shared resources, sexuality, death, and transformation, including your partner's money, inheritances, taxes, and the psyche. Energies here illuminate your extent for intimacy and regeneration.

- **9th House:** This house rules higher learning, philosophy, religion, travel, and mental expansion. Energies here influence your quest for meaning, moral beliefs, and experiences that transcend your mindset.

- **10th House:** Status, achievement, and public reputation manifest in the 10th house. It represents your career path, social standing, and your role in the larger community. Energies here influence your ambitions and public persona.

- **11th House:** Friendships, group involvements, humanitarian concerns, and long-term goals manifest in the 11th house. Energies here influence your social consciousness.

- **12th House:** The final house governs the subconscious mind, self-undoing, confinement, and spiritual transcendence. Energies here determine your shadows, karmic baggage, and mystical and intuitive powers.

Astrology and Soul Contracts

The interpretation of pre-birth agreements through astrology is a complicated and subjective process. However, in the astrological community, special planetary alignments point to pre-agreements you made before incarnation. These alignments are:

- **Saturn Returns:** Every 27 to 30 years, Saturn returns to the same position it held when you were born. This return is a performance review, where the universe demands that you face the music and take a long, brutal look at the choices you've made and the responsibilities you've taken on. It's a time for reckoning, a period where you're asked to confront your fears and limitations and step into your power. As expected, many people aren't ecstatic about this because there will be issues that can't be ignored – crises that will force you to grow up. However, there's nothing to be afraid of. Saturn's return is your chance to shed the old skin and become the person you're truly meant to be. It's a time to honor the soul-level commitments you made and gain the wisdom that comes from facing your fears.

- **North Node and South Node:** The North and South nodes are points in your astrological birth chart representing where you're headed (North node) and where you've been (South node). The South node represents your past lives, the talents you incarnated with, and comfortable behavioral patterns. It's a well-worn path that feels familiar to you. The energies in your South node show the qualities and skills you've developed over many lifetimes.

While they can be a bonus in this lifetime, they can become crutches or limitations if you get stuck in them. The South node is your comfort zone and the habits that keep you from growing. Alternatively, the North node points to your soul's destiny and the areas where you're meant to stretch and evolve. The energies in your North node show you the qualities and life experiences you agreed to develop if you hope to fulfill your life purpose in this lifetime. They are there to push you out of your comfort zone.

- **Chiron:** Chiron was a centaur in Greek mythology – and a healer. Ironically, he also carried two painful wounds that could never fully heal: one *psychological* and the other *physical*. This contradiction – being a healer with an unhealed wound – is the essence of Chiron's astrological symbolism. Chiron's placement reveals the areas where you have the potential to become a wounded healer, where your pain can become the source of your greatest gifts. Working with this energy is not for the weak because it requires facing your wounds, feeling the full depth of your pain, and resisting the temptation to numb yourself. Chiron's energy teaches you to acknowledge your imperfections and to love yourself, flaws and all.

Planetary Alignments and What They Mean

Contrary to what you might think, planets and their influences are not separate and compartmentalized. Their energies affect the collective consciousness. These collective shifts are strongest during transits, retrogrades, and eclipses.

Transits

A transit is when a planet moves from one point in the sky to another. These movements are unavoidable, and as the planet moves, it passes through particular points in your birth chart. These pit stops always come bearing gifts for you and the collective. For example, Jupiter could be transiting over your 10th house, your career house. During this transit, you may notice expansion, new possibilities, or growth in your work life. Jupiter's energy (luck, abundance, and optimism) activates and influences your career as it passes over it.

Collective transits happen when a planet moves into a new zodiac sign, not only a point in your birth chart. Everyone is affected because its energy shifts the collective consciousness and experiences. For example, when Saturn enters Capricorn, generally, there is a greater emphasis on structure, responsibility, and the need for sustainable long-term solutions. Businesses and governments may tighten their belts, and people feel pressured to get serious about their goals and commitments. Or when disruptive Uranus transits into Aquarius, there's social change, technological advancements, innovation, and independence. If you're paying attention, you'll notice major cultural, political, or scientific breakthroughs during these transits.

Transits are not spontaneous; they can be predicted with near-perfect accuracy, so anyone can prepare for and harness these energies' influences when they happen.

Retrogrades

When a planet appears to be moving backward in the sky, this is called retrograde, and it happens regularly for all the planets. The most popular one is Mercury retrograde. During these 3 to 4-week periods a few times a year, communications, technology, and travel can get weird. Emails get lost, your computer crashes, your flight gets delayed, among other things. Mercury retrograde is a time to slow down, be extra mindful, and avoid making major decisions if possible.

Venus retrograde is another popular one that happens every 1.5 years or so. When the planet of love, beauty, and values seems to move backward, it's time to reassess your relationships, artistic projects, and what truly matters to you. Old flames may return, or you may need to renegotiate the terms of a current relationship.

The outer planets – Jupiter, Saturn, Uranus, Neptune, and Pluto, also have retrogrades that last for months. These longer retrogrades are an invitation to go inward and re-evaluate the big-picture themes and structures in your life. For example, a Saturn retrograde wants you to take a hard look at your responsibilities and commitments. Retrogrades, as frustrating as they are, are not punishment. They are for reflection and course correction. Everyone is better off using these energies to review, rework, and revise.

Eclipses

Spiritually, eclipses signal the end of one chapter and the beginning of another. A solar eclipse, when the moon passes between the sun and the Earth, can bring sudden changes like the end of a relationship or a new beginning. It is a very uncertain time, but this disruption is necessary to clear the way for positive transformation. Lunar eclipses, when the Earth passes between the sun and moon, are more associated with emotional awareness, intuition, and release. Secrets will come to the surface, or you may feel the need to let go of what no longer serves you. An eclipse interrupts the normal rhythms of the sun and moon, causing a cosmic reset. It is asking you to let go and trust the process. Trust that what's ahead is always better than what you leave behind.

What Is Your North Node?

North Node	Meaning
Aries	You're here to learn to be brave, to take the lead, to stand up for yourself, and to put your needs first.
Taurus	Your destiny is to find joy in the physical world and to appreciate beauty, comfort, and worldly pleasures.
Gemini	Your purpose is to be a curious, adaptable learner. You're here to experience new things, communicate better, and see things from many perspectives.
Cancer	Your destiny involves developing your emotional intelligence. You're here to create a safe, supportive home and care for the people in your life.
Leo	You're here to shine, find joy in self-expression, and lead confidently.
Virgo	Your destiny is to perfect your skills, pay attention to details, and serve others.

North Node	Meaning
Libra	You're here to learn to compromise and bring people together.
Scorpio	Your destiny involves the mysteries of life, death, and rebirth, as well as facing your fears.
Sagittarius	You're here to be a truth-seeker, visionary, and free spirit.
Capricorn	Your destiny is to develop discipline, responsibility, and practical mastery of the material world.
Aquarius	Your purpose is to be an innovative, humanitarian, and unconventional thinker. You're here to contribute to the greater good.
Pisces	Your destiny involves compassion, spirituality, and a connection to the universal flow. You're here to transcend the ego, surrender to your intuition, and serve as a healer or mystic.

Chapter 5: Exploring the Akashic Records to Find Your Mission

An infinite mega library containing the complete record of every soul's journey through time and space seems suspiciously unrealistic, but the idea is not as far-fetched as logic would claim. This library is not fiction. It is called the Akashic records. The Akashic records are a massive catalog comprising the past, present, and future of all beings, events, thoughts, and emotions that have or will ever exist.

The Akashic Records are like a vast library that holds the imprint of the soul's experiences.[15]

The word *"Akasha"* originates from the ancient Sanskrit language, meaning *"aether," "primary substance,"* or *"source of all that exists."* The Akashic records are encoded within this fundamental, primordial substance that runs through the entire universe. Like how the ocean holds the history and movement of every wave, current, and living sea creature, the Akashic records hold the complete energetic imprint of every soul's experiences, thoughts, and actions.

There are no known coordinates to this library. It is not located in a physical place but instead exists as a non-physical plane – a multi-dimensional database. Many believe that the Akashic records can only be accessed through altered states of consciousness, like in deep meditation, channeling, or working with a professional Akashic records reader.

Akashic records shape or form is evident in many religious and philosophical traditions worldwide. In Hinduism and Buddhism, the Akashic records are a basal component of the universe. The ancient Egyptians spoke of the Hall of Records, a hidden chamber underneath the Sphinx that contained the secrets of human civilization. In Judeo-Christian traditions, the Book of Life mentioned in the Bible is sometimes interpreted as a reference to the Akashic records.

According to Hindu cosmology, the universe is not a cluster of disparate and independent entities. It is an infinite integrated system governed by the principles of Brahman, the supreme, all-encompassing reality. The Akashic records are the manifestation of Brahman's eternal, all-pervading consciousness to Hindus. The Akashic records are not only a passive information bank but an active, living entity and a conduit for the exchange of energy, wisdom, and spiritual understanding. Every thought, action, and experience that has or will ever occur is recorded and stored within this intelligent, interconnected network.

The Hindus believe that access to the Akashic records is not limited to a select few but is everyone's birthright. However, the depth and clarity of your connection to this sacred place rests on your spiritual development, intuition, and receptivity to the cosmic energies that flow through everything. This library is essential to the Hindu concept of karma because it contains a detailed record of your past lives, including the actions, thoughts, and experiences that led to your existence. Access to this library means that you can finally understand your karmic patterns and the lessons you have yet to learn on your spiritual journey.

Akashic Records and Your Soul Contract

Since the Akashic records hold every piece of information on your soul's evolution, then the details of your soul contract are somewhere in that gigantic archive. You could go a step further and say that soul contracts are drafted using the information from this library. For the most part, it functions like a regular public library, except instead of books, you can borrow the complete energetic history and future potentials of every incarnation you've had. So, it makes sense that when your soul contract was being created, you "borrowed" the relevant files containing all the necessary details about your soul's past.

Fortunately, these records aren't only accessible in nonphysical form. Humans can and have reached into these metaphysical archives to retrieve information about their soul's journey. The information within the Akashic records is objective and impartial, reflecting nothing but the truth about a person's soul journey. It's not filtered through anyone's opinions or agendas. It's the pure, unvarnished truth about your soul's experiences. So, you wouldn't have to worry about anyone's preconceptions or judgments distorting your discoveries.

The Akashic records sound like a place where anyone, regardless of race, gender, or religion, would want to visit. Can you imagine all the information it contains about you and the *"you's"* that ever existed? Were you rich in your previous life? Were you a man or a woman? Did you fall in love? Were you a queen? How many former lives have you had? What was your first life? What did you look like? Who wouldn't want to know?

This is the backstage pass of all backstage passes. However, an Akashic reading should be about more than satisfying your curiosity about the past. Somewhere in those records is the information to keep your present-day choices and actions in alignment with your soul's highest good. You will understand why certain things happened the way they did and why you had to go through your experiences.

Clarity and self-discovery of this magnitude may not be as easy as you think. What you learn might be uncomfortable or painful to face. You may find past life traumas, unhealed wounds, or crippling terrors that have been silently influencing your reality. Are you brave enough to find out? Will you run away from your shadow? Are you ready to take responsibility for your life, or do you want to forever be a victim of circumstance?

How to Access the Akashic Records

The Akashic records are open to everyone. It does not discriminate, is not exclusive, and it does not judge. The only requirements are intention, respect, and receptiveness.

There is more than one way to connect with this library. You can use:

Guided Meditations and Visualizations

This is the most common technique for accessing the Akashic records. Guided meditations put you in a relaxed state. Your conscious mind quiets and your intuition becomes more receptive to energetic downloads.

During a guided meditation, you might be led through a sacred space in your mind's eye. This could be a library, hallway, or field. As you connect more with this imaginary place and the images become clearer, you might receive downloads - information, wisdom, or guidance - directly from Akasha.

The physical world is an illusion, a distorted reflection of higher dimensions. The mind has enough power to transcend the physical limitations of its earthly vessel temporarily. It's all about intention. With the right spiritual practices, the mind can do almost anything, including bridge the gap between the physical and the ethereal, where the Akashic records are found.

Prayer and Intention

Another tried and true way to reach the Akashic records is through prayer and intention. Setting a clear intention to connect with the records sends a request to the universe. It invokes help and direction from the Akashic guides.

Prayer can take many forms. You can say a few genuine words or perform more structured invocations. Some people have used affirmations, such as "I now open myself to the wisdom of the Akashic records" or "I ask the Akashic guides to share their knowledge with me." The exact wording is not as important as the sincerity and devotion you bring to the practice.

Akashic Reading

If you can't access your Akashic records on your own, you can hire a professional Akashic reader to be the bridge between you and this space. An Akashic reader has mastered the skills to consciously access the Akashic records. They have undergone extensive training and spiritual development to hone their intuition and learn the protocols for respectfully and safely entering the Akashic space. Through meditation, energy work, pendulums, tarot, and other metaphysical means, they can channel information, messages, and wisdom relevant to your life's purpose, lessons, and relationships.

There's no such thing as a "wrong" question during an Akashic reading unless you try to access someone else's records. You're not allowed. Only you can access your records – and only with your explicit permission. Your reading might not make sense to you right away, but go with it, trust your intuition, and use your discernment. Ultimately, an Akashic reading gives clarity. It does not confuse you, so ask as many questions as you want. They are your records, and you are entitled to their wisdom.

Journaling and Inquiry

Journaling can also grant you access to the Akashic records. It sounds too simple, doesn't it? Sometimes, it can be. You'll need a book to write down your questions or areas you would like to investigate. This creates a tangible focal point for the Akashic guides to work with. Then, set an intention to connect with the library. Responses could come as intuitive realizations, feelings, or impressions. Write down whatever pops into your head, related or seemingly unrelated. Don't overthink anything, don't edit or censor yourself, just keep writing. Have patience and stay open-minded. The answers you want may not arrive in the form you expect, but they will come if you remain receptive and keep the communication lines open.

Dowsing

For this, it's better to use a pendulum, not dowsing rods, especially if you've never done it before. How it works is quite straightforward. Hold the pendulum, set your intention, and ask your question. In response, the pendulum will move. The movements' direction and pattern are answers, depending on what each movement means to you. You could set the intention that a forward swing means "yes," side-to-side means "no," and a circle means "I don't know." The only downside to this is that you can only receive yes or no answers from the Akashic records, meaning your questions must be *specific.*

Use a pendulum for dowsing.[16]

Channeling

Channeling is a controversial practice, and for good reason. As a channel, you're a living, breathing microphone for a multidimensional entity. You're trusting and surrendering your physical form to it. That's a big deal, and it is not a decision to be made lightly. You're essentially inviting a spiritual being, with its thoughts, personality, and agenda, to take over your body and speak through you. That's a lot of power to hand over, and it's understandable why some people feel uneasy about it.

Channeling has been around for centuries. Entire traditions are based around it and they all agree on one thing: it must be done with proper care, intention, and respect. You're not merely opening the door to some random entity – you're establishing a sacred connection with a higher intelligence that must be treated with the utmost respect. In this case, you're channeling the Akashic records, which requires great spiritual maturity. You must let go of your ego, your preconceptions, and your need for control. However, if you do it right, you get an experience that could be life-changing.

Benefits of Accessing the Akashic Records

- **Clarity on life's challenges and recurring patterns**

  Sometimes, clarity is all a person could ever want. Life is complicated enough without problems that refuse to go away. You're trying to plug a leak in a dam, only to have it spring up somewhere else. Wouldn't you want to know why you keep getting into the same unhealthy relationships? Why do you feel stuck in a career you only need to pay your bills? The answers are in your Akashic records. It could be that your patterns stretch back generations or lifetimes, or your purpose is connected to a talent you never took seriously. The Akashic records can give you understanding and direction to break free from the cycles that have kept you stuck.

- **Unresolved karma and how to heal them**

  The Akashic records can help you see into your past lives and the patterns that have carried over into your current incarnation. Karma is the universal law of cause and effect. So, if you have access to your past lives, you can understand the karmic patterns influencing your current life, especially unresolved karmas, which are the negative or unresolved incidents from past lives that will manifest until they are dealt with. For example, you may have participated in a betrayal or caused an abandonment wound in a past life. This unresolved karma could manifest in your life as failed relationships, trust issues, or commitment issues. When you understand this, you can begin to heal and release the emotional and energetic patterns that have driven these behaviors instead of going in circles for the rest of your life. When you heal karma, the effect of that singular act spreads through the collective consciousness and heals a part of humanity as a whole. Remember, everything is connected.

- **Understand your soul's purpose**

  Every person has a reason for incarnating, a contribution only they can make during their lifetime. The problem is that everyone forgets what it is as soon as they are born and spend their entire life figuring it out. Nobody starts a mystery novel from the middle because you need the first few chapters for context. You know there's a bigger story at play, but now, you have to piece it together as you read. The Akashic records can show you where you're supposed to go and the clues to get there. You don't have to force yourself into a predetermined path anymore because you'll know, with unwavering certainty, that you are here for a reason and that you matter in the grand scheme of things.

- **Strengthen your spiritual connection and intuition**

The Akashic records hold the answers to all of life's questions - information, guidance, and wisdom far beyond your lived experiences and your logical mind. Your intuition is the key to everything. It is the thread that links you to everything else. Information travels up and down this thread with or without your awareness. It is one way to receive information or energetic downloads from within and outside the 3D. Your spiritual connection might get you access to the Akashic records, but it is your intuition that interprets and integrates the responses. Your intuition bridges the gap between the seen and the unseen, the known and the unknowable. It is the language your soul speaks and understands. Your job is to listen closely. When you even attempt to access the Akashic records, you listen to your intuition, and the more you listen, the better you become at recognizing it. Soon it becomes second nature, and you live in awareness of your connection to everything.

Access Your Soul's Records

1. You'll need to be in a comfortable position, seated or lying down.

2. Close your eyes and disconnect your awareness from the outside world.

3. Imagine your physical body is dissolving, becoming porous and permeable. Feel yourself becoming a glowing, energetic field, a swirling vortex of light and information.

4. Feel this field expanding until the boundaries between your consciousness and the universal consciousness dissolve. You are no longer a separate self. You are one with a unified field of pure potential.

5. As you surrender to this expansive awareness, you should pick up on discreet vibrations and frequencies. These energetic signatures are the Akashic records. See it in your mind's eye as a holographic matrix, inseparable from reality.

6. Imagine your energy field becoming a transmitter, a receiver, an encoder, and a decoder of this network. Your consciousness is now a tuning fork, attuned to the exact frequencies coming from this matrix.

7. See your energy field transform and take on a new geometric configuration. It is now an iridescent dodecahedron – the sacred, 12-sided shape that represents holistic interconnectedness and the highest consciousness. This crystalline structure is your portal, your interface with the Akashic space.

8. As you hold this visualization, imagine the dodecahedron spinning, vibrating, generating sound, and beaming with light.

9. Sink into this sensory experience and release expectations or preconceptions of what is happening. Your rational mind should be in reverent surrender so your intuition can take the lead.

10. Remain in this state until you notice what you intuitively know a library is materializing around you. It is not a physical space but a multidimensional intelligent matrix filled with information. The volumes on the shelves are not made of paper but of light, sound, and pure coded consciousness.

11. As you turn your attention to this library, notice that the "books" are opening and closing on their own, and you receive data snippets and cascades of symbolic meaning. Don't be afraid; remain calm and open.

12. If you have a particular question, hold that intention in your mind. Let your intuition guide you as you reach out and touch the pulsing, holographic archives.

13. Wait and pay attention; the information you seek will come to you in ways that transcend linear thinking.

14. You may receive a vision, a feeling, or a realization. You may hear whispers or feel an energetic imprint. Trust that Akasha is responding to you in the way it knows you will understand.

15. When you are done, show gratitude for the wisdom and understanding you've received.

16. Imagine your dodecahedral form receding and your consciousness gradually returning to your physical vessel.

17. Breathe in deeply and breathe out, then open your eyes.

Chapter 6: Connecting with Guides and Higher Beings for Clarity

Spirit guides as a concept is a highly misunderstood aspect of spirituality. Are they real? Are they not? On one side of the debate are those who believe in the existence of spirit guides – benevolent, non-physical entities assigned to support the soul's growth and mission. To them, spirit guides are real, tangible presences.

On the other side are the skeptics. Spirit guides are nothing more than a product of the human imagination – a comforting fantasy people create to cope with life and general misfortune. To them, non-physical entities guiding and assisting humanity are not supported by scientific evidence. They cannot be considered "real" in the conventional sense.

However, there's a third side. This group sees it as a personal, subjective experience that may or may not be for everyone. They'd rather approach the concept curiously and discernibly, not with blind belief or outright dismissal.

Connecting with your guides will bring you clarity.[17]

No matter what side you're on, the belief in a supernatural being that guides and protects humans has a place in every religion and twice as many traditions. There are guardian angels in Islam and Christianity, spirit animals in indigenous cultures, and ascended masters in Eastern philosophies. The Hindus have Ishta devata, there's an entire pantheon of gods and goddesses for the ancient Egyptians, Africans look to their ancestors, and Jews believe in maggids.

It is human nature to believe in something greater, something that can provide mentorship, protection, and a connection to the divine, especially where confusion, grief, or an existential crisis exists.

Spirit guides, to believers, are compassionate, immaterial entities that exist on a higher dimension and have a nuanced understanding of the human experience and the universal principles governing existence. They are manifestations of divine energy, acting as intermediaries between the physical and spiritual worlds. People have associated them with many archetypes or symbolic representations, like animals, ancestors, or angels, to better receive and understand their energies and messages.

Spirit guides provide clarity, direction, and wisdom when there is uncertainty, transition, or personal growth. They do this with intuitive nudges, synchronicities, and, sometimes, direct communication.

You are more than just your physical body. You have an eternal, non-physical form – the soul, which is connected to a higher intelligence or consciousness. The spirit guides are responsible for the soul. Their assistance cannot be forced or replicated. It happens organically in divine timing.

Types of Spirit Guides

Guardian Angels

Guardian angels are spiritual beings that, according to many beliefs, are entrusted to watch over and protect humans. For example, Christians believe in guardian angels because biblical passages imply that God appointed angels to watch over and guide people. Psalms 91:11 says, *"For he will command his angels concerning you to guard you in all your ways."*

In Islam, guardian angels are called *"Malak."* These angels record a person's deeds, good and bad, and intercede on their behalf with God. Surah Ar-Ra'd (13:11): *"For each [person] are successive [angels] before and behind him who protect him by the decree of Allah."* Every human has a guardian angel, a spirit being walking beside them, so they don't have to go through life alone. Believers say they have experienced their guardian angel's presence, especially in the form of unexpected help. For them, guardian angels are a source of strength and protection, even though you can't physically see them.

Ancestral Spirits

Cultures that don't see their dead as truly gone but as having transitioned to a different dimension as ancestral spirits. They maintain a connection to their dead for continuity and spiritual support despite death. You could see your ancestors in dreams or visions or feel them intuitively if your connection is strong enough. Many cultures venerate their ancestors. For example, in Africa and Asia, families keep altars or shrines dedicated to their ancestors. They say prayers, offer gifts, and perform rituals to honor their memory, ask for blessings, and draw upon the wisdom, protection, and spiritual energy of those who lived before.

Ascended Masters: Ascended Masters are people who, through their unrelenting dedication and spiritual evolution, have conquered the limitations of the physical world and reached enlightenment and mastery. Described as wise and compassionate beings who have become one with the divine, they work as guides and inspirations for those seeking spiritual understanding.

The title *"Ascended Master"* goes back to Theosophy and the I AM Movement. This movement's teachings maintain that Ascended Masters were once ordinary humans who transcended the human experience. They are no longer bound by the physical world – yet remain connected to it by choice for humanity's sake. Believers say the Ascended Masters work behind the scenes, sending love, healing, and guidance to those who are open to receiving them. They are living examples of what is possible when a person fully embraces their spiritual path. Some of the most popular Ascended Masters are Krishna, Jesus, Buddha, and Saint Germain.

Higher Self

The higher self is the true, pure version of you within the human vessel. It is the wiser, more expansive part of self that is connected to something greater than ego. As your normal, day-to-day consciousness worries about things like your physical needs and base desires, the higher self sees past this limited perspective. This part of you is already aligned with your highest values, your intuition, and your spirituality.

The higher self has been called the *"divine spark"* because it is not separate from the divine. It is the divine within you. It is a guiding light that knows what is true and good. You don't have to earn your higher self or search for it; it is already there, steadily conspiring with the universe for your highest good, even on days when it doesn't feel like it.

Animal Guides

Nobody said spirit guides have to be humanoid. Cultures as old as civilization have believed in animal guides. They believe everyone has one or more animals that are spiritually connected to them. These spirit animals have peculiar qualities, characteristics, and energies crucial to their person's path. Many cultures maintain that your spirit animal chooses you and then makes its presence known through signs, dreams, or synchronistic sightings of the physical animal in the real world.

There could be a bird you feel weirdly drawn to for no obvious reason, or you keep randomly seeing pictures of the same animal everywhere. These experiences are usually interpreted as your spirit animal trying to get your attention and inviting you to learn from its wisdom. Animal guides are quite protective of their person, watching over you and fighting for you.

Do Spirit Guides Interfere with Free Will?

Spirit guides are not enforcers. They do not control or manipulate you. Despite being free from the limitations that humans are bound by, they only guide, support, and lend perspectives that could help you. The decisions are always yours to make. They are every wise old mentor in the movies who gives the young hero invaluable advice and encouragement but never forces them to do anything. Your guides will share their suggestions and foresight with you, but they'll respect your autonomy to decide what feels right.

They are called guides for a reason. They are not here to live your life for you. If anything, their influence is subtle. They don't shout orders or unexpectedly take over your decision-making. They don't want you to blindly follow their instructions. They want you to develop your confidence and hone your discernment. They are most helpful when they inspire you to think for yourself, and that's all they want to do – help.

There may be times when your guides try to steer you in a direction that doesn't feel right. In these moments, you can go your own way and do whatever you want. They'll never punish or force you to comply. That's the beauty of the spirit guide-human relationship; it's a partnership built on mutual respect and trust.

Spirit guides can help you understand the lessons you are incarnated to learn. Assuming your lesson is about body dysmorphia, you could run into a total stranger at a coffee shop who, without knowing your story, tells you exactly what you need to hear, and the conversation starts a domino effect that changes your life. Your guides understand that life isn't only an intellectual exercise – your emotions and intuition are also involved. They see the big picture, the overarching themes, the lessons you've learned, and the greater purpose that underlies your most painful memories. They pick up on your heart's whispers that you are too afraid to hear and amplify them right back at you in a language they know you'll understand. Spirit guides are not omniscient; they don't have all the answers, but they do what they can to lead you away from pitfalls and in the right direction. You have free will, yet there is always more than one right direction.

Signs of Spirit Guide Communication

- **Gut Feelings**

Spirit guides love to communicate through intuitive nudges or gut feelings – those sudden hunches, not-so-random fleeting thoughts, or strong feelings that something is right or wrong, even if you can't logically explain why. Your guides send you messages by plugging into your subconscious to give advice, warnings, or clarity. These intuitive hits pop up out of nowhere without a rational explanation for where they came from or why. The messages are typically confirmations, realizations, or an urge to do something, avoid a situation, or pay closer attention to something.

Your relationship with your spirit guides depends on how well you can recognize, decipher, and trust what they tell you. Don't worry too much if you initially dismiss or doubt the messages, especially if your mind can't immediately make sense of them. In your defense, a bulk of it only makes sense in hindsight.

Some people need only one confirmation that they're not going crazy. Other people need as many as they can get, but none of that matters. What matters is the faith you have in your intuition, a faith that is hard-won and gives you the confidence to trust your spirit guides. The stronger your faith, the clearer the messages become, forming a positive feedback loop. Your intuition guides you, and your spirit guides reinforce your faith in your intuition by sending more easily recognizable signs. The signs have always been easily recognizable, but you have only started paying attention.

- **Synchronicities**

Another sign of a spirit guide's presence is uncanny, borderline supernatural coincidences or meaningful coincidences that are too perfect to be random. This could show up in your life as seeing the same number, symbol, or image in the most unrelated contexts, almost as if it is following you everywhere. It could also be a chance encounter with a person at just the right time or a piece of information showing up precisely when you need it.

These are called synchronicities. They aren't random happenstance – they're orchestrated by your guides to affirm your faith, to prepare you for something, or as an attempt to redirect you. There's so much happening in your life, so sometimes you need a little help or a reminder. Your guides know what to give you and when. Also, they have a sense of humor. These so-called coincidences could be their idea of a joke, a little wink from the other side. Hence, you must pay attention so that you get the joke and everyone has a good laugh.

Sometimes, it's your cue to stop, think, and figure out the message's meaning. What are they drawing your attention to? What is there to learn from this? What are you not seeing? You interpret synchronicities through presence and curiosity.

• Messages Through Dreams or Meditation

Your spirit guides have many ways to get in touch with you. One way is through your dreams and when you're in a meditative state. In the dream state, your guides can meet you directly to give you wisdom or guidance that feels crystal clear, even if the imagery is a tad symbolic or metaphorical. They could use anything from vivid symbolism and poetic metaphors to full-blown narratives that feel deserving of a sequel. It conveys their vital message. When you wake up, you're left with clarity, inspiration, or the desire to act based on your dream.

It's the same during meditation. Your guides can reveal themselves using sensations, thoughts, or epiphanies. The messages can be straightforward – a clear instruction or a vision. As long as you are receptive during meditation, you create an opening for your guides to meet you halfway.

• Physical Sensations

Spirit guides reach out through physical sensations. You could suddenly feel warm or get a tingling like electricity pulsating in a part of your body – mostly around the crown, third eye, heart, or solar plexus chakras. Some people say they have felt a literal touch, a breeze, or a presence beside them. You don't necessarily have to feel them; you can smell them, and your intuition knows what they mean. Physical cues are essential clues that your guides are near or actively trying to communicate.

Contacting Your Spirit Guides

Meditation

If you got a dollar for every time you were asked to meditate, how rich would you be? You hear it a lot, don't you? It's been mentioned a handful of times in this book already, but it is all they say it is. If you want to connect with your spirit guides, one of the best ways is meditation. Modern life has made the mind too loud and too busy. Life is so distracting that stillness seems far outside your comfort zone, but in stillness, you find the channels that connect you to your guides. The entire point of meditation is stillness and mindful awareness. When there is nothing but awareness, you can hear and feel them. They've been there the whole time; their messages just got lost in the noise. You need to relax and silence the noise, be present, breathe, and let them speak to you.

Meditation provides you with focus to reach a higher plane.[18]

Setting Intentions

This applies to anything you hope to succeed in. You plan before you execute. You think before you speak. You set goals and then achieve them. You set a clear intention, and then you contact your spirit guides. You could set an intention by saying, "I need help with so-and-so." Don't demand anything or try to force a response; that rarely works. Show genuine respect and gratitude, then listen. Your guides are more than happy to respond to your sincere invitation to communicate.

Automatic Writing

Write down questions or requests for your spirit guides on paper or in your notes app if you prefer to type. Take a few deep breaths, relax, and let the answers flow from your intuition. Whatever comes through, write it down. Don't worry about it making sense; you have plenty of time to figure that out. When you're done writing, leave it alone; don't look at it. Give your mind time to relax. If you have other things to do, go ahead. Return to your scribblings much later and see if the messages make sense then.

Divination

Spirit guides speak through oracle cards, pendulums, runes, and other symbolic tools. Divination is usually the go-to for multidimensional messages, but it is only one of many channels. Always center yourself and set your intention before you start so that your guides come in clearly to work with you. Trust your intuition; professional diviners do. They know the symbol's meanings they work with. However, they know it is more than that. You could be looking at the three of swords in a Tarot deck, and your message has nothing to do with the card's official meaning. Your message might be in the imagery, the colors, or an isolated symbol on the card in the deck. Your guides are trusting you to use your intuition to decipher the messages. They know you can, and deep down, you know it, too.

Ask Your Spirit Guides About Your Soul Mission

1. Go somewhere quiet and comfortable where you won't be disturbed.

2. Light a candle or incense to set the mood.

3. Breathe in deeply and breathe out three times. Feel your body relax.

4. Imagine walking through a beautiful garden. The air is fresh, and there's not a single worry on your mind.

5. As you continue down the path, quietly call on your spirit guides until you sense another presence with you.

6. Look ahead and see your spirit guide materializing from nothing. Their energy is so warm and loving that it instantly puts you at ease. This is a being you know you can trust with all your heart.

7. Walk to your guide and greet them. Thank them for coming.

8. Gently explain that you've come seeking advice about your soul's higher purpose. Ask your questions, all at once or one by one – it's up to you.

9. Walk with them as they telepathically share the answers to your questions. They will speak if they want or need to.

10. Concentrate with an open heart and trust that the information they share is divinely inspired. If you have follow-up questions, don't hesitate to ask them. They're here to give you as much clarity as possible.

11. When the exchange feels complete, you'll see a fork in the road. Thank them again, pick a path, any path, and walk. This time, alone.

12. Stay in this garden as long as you want until you are ready to rejoin the world.

13. Open your eyes.

Chapter 7: The Role of Karma and Past Lives

When a pebble is dropped into a still pond, the initial plop disturbs the water surface where it makes contact. Then, it ripples and expands from the center. These ripples are the karmic effects of the original drop.

Karma is the ripple effects of life.[19]

Karma is an ancient Eastern belief. It is a spiritual principle that relies on cause and effect. Karma teaches that your actions, thoughts, and intentions in this life can and will affect your future in this life or the next. Everything in the universe is interconnected, and your choices and behaviors, conscious or unconscious, cause a ripple in time extending beyond your immediate circumstances.

To understand karma, first understand that your destiny is in your hands. Every decision you make, every word you speak, and every action you execute sets in motion consequences that will shape the future, and not only yours. This single belief is why you must be mindful and intentional in everything you do; you are largely responsible for the direction and progression of many lives, especially yours.

Karma teaches compassion and empathy. Your actions have the power to change other people's lives for better or worse. If you understand this, you'll be more inclined to behave carefully and considerately. These changes, good or bad, don't happen immediately, but when they do happen, it's hard to tell what led to what. The laws in charge of this system are far above your pay grade.

Humans can't directly trace the actions that caused the effect. You think you know, but you don't. You're better off keeping your eye on all the dominoes in a massive, almost eternal arrangement, which is impossible. You might see how a tile knocks over the next one. Still, eventually, everything happens so fast and all at once that it's impossible to follow every domino as it falls. There are too many variables at play – the weight of the tiles, the angle they're placed, or the possibility of your 7-year-old sister dashing straight through your arrangement. However, even though you can't 100% predict or control every outcome, it doesn't mean the system is meaningless or that your arrangement doesn't matter. The "effect" to the "cause" could take years or lifetimes to come to fruition, but uncertainty shouldn't stop you from choosing compassion and kindness.

Karma Is Not Punishment or Reward

Karma has become a bad word. People hear it and immediately think there's a scorekeeper in the sky doling out rewards and punishments based on behavior. When you touch a hot stove, you get burned, don't you? Would you say that the stove punished you? Probably not. It's what you get when touching a hot stove. Would you call getting burned karma? Maybe, maybe not.

Karma is not an external force that plays judge, jury, and consequences. It is nothing but a feedback loop. It is a mirror that points your actions back at you. There is no life without choice – and every time you choose, it leads to one thing that leads to another and another, and somehow, the initial "plop" makes its way back to you. Your decision, good or bad, becomes the lesson you need to learn and grow.

Fixating on a scoring system, where virtuous deeds earn you points and misdeeds land you in the "bad karma" column, will cause you to miss the point. You'll miss the point by trying to rack up good karma points in a bid to avoid punishment. The point is in the details. When you think you're being punished, ask yourself, "What is this trying to teach me?" There are lessons to learn from even the positive fruits of your labor.

The most valuable lessons come wrapped in "good karma." When things are going your way, and you're on a winning streak, your first thought might be to pat yourself on the back and think you're doing it right. You are, but that's not all there is to it. The temptation is to be so content in the satisfaction from your achievements that your good karma becomes a validation from the universe. Everything is going well, so you think you have it all figured out, or you think your good fortune is proof of your superiority. Again, you're missing the point. Karma isn't a scoreboard.

Your successes can show you your blind spots, but if you get too attached to the results, you lose the lessons that came with them. Success exposes areas where you're stronger but also areas where there may still be room for growth. There is wisdom in humility, and remember that your wins can teach you something important about yourself.

Karma and Past Incarnations

Reincarnation and past lives are true for many people, even if they can't explain how or prove it. The déjà vu, the prophetic dreams, strange phobias, and uncharacteristic talents suggest that some souls have lived before and have accumulated knowledge and skills over many lifetimes.

You picked up skills or hobbies with surprising ease, as if you were born doing it. Also, you have fears or phobias in this life that you don't understand. For all you know, you could've been executed for expressing yourself in a past life, which has carried over into this lifetime. Talent and trauma are not bound by time and space.

Also, karma is not bound by time and space. The seeds you plant in one lifetime can sprout decades or even centuries later, and the seeds they produce can continue to spread and grow long after you're gone. Until you stop reincarnating, your current life will have trickles from your past incarnations. These trickles can be unconscious memories and imprints from another life to karma. Each incarnation comes with lessons. Some lessons you learned well, and you carry that wisdom with you. Others were missed or learned imperfectly, so you struggle with the same things, over and over, in different forms.

Past Life Regression

Past life regression is an exercise in hypnosis through which you directly access and consciously step into your previous incarnations. You get to see yourself in a different body and life. You get to live as they lived, feel what they felt, and see how you could've done better. Access to these past life lessons you missed – these karmas – frees you from the negative cycles and limiting beliefs that have stuck to you, like Velcro, because now you understand and know how to heal. A woman who was abused in a past life can finally understand and heal her commitment issues. A man haunted by memories of war and violence can finally discover the reason for his anger issues.

Looking far into the past sounds fun. Anyone would be curious. However, curiosity is only half of it. A past life regression could root out memories that are terrifying to confront, memories better left in another lifetime. Regression therapists believe this discomfort is a necessary part of healing, but that doesn't make it easier. Nobody will blame you for wanting to keep those skeletons firmly in the closet, locked away where they can't haunt you anymore. But the price you pay for avoidance is far greater than the temporary discomfort of regression. Past life regression is a chance to alchemize your painful pasts into self-actualization and enlightenment. Facing and integrating the unlearned lessons from your previous lives, you become a whole, authentic version of yourself in this life.

A trained hypnotherapist or regression therapist will guide you into and through the process using gentle, meditative prompts. First, you'll go into a dissociative state, then into a liminal space between waking and sleeping, where the subconscious becomes more accessible.

Once you're in this altered state, the therapist will invite you to recall impressions, sensations, and images from a past life, often starting with the moment of your death. The things that are exposed can be eerily vivid and detailed – the sights, sounds, and physical sensations from another time and place. People have vividly seen clothing, architecture, and family from their former lives. The emotions you'll experience can be as real and poignant as any you feel in your current incarnation.

You may be disoriented as you are transported to an entirely different era with a different identity and life experiences. The detail and authenticity can feel more like a memory than imagination. You could be looking through the eyes of a young peasant girl in medieval Europe or a Spartan on a battlefield. The visceral sensations – the scratches from rough fabric, wound stings, and exhaustion – can feel startlingly real, and these sensations come with emotions, positive and negative, such as joy, sorrow, fear, and anger. People have wept uncontrollably over a long-lost love or were shaken to their core in terror as they relived their death, but, like every spiritual experience, there's more.

The healer from your medieval past reincarnated as you, a nurse or midwife in this life, or the betrayal you suffered in another life could help you understand your trust issues and perhaps find peace. Every lifetime is another chance to integrate the lessons of the past and grow beyond them. Karma has led you to this life, where you have nothing but an opportunity to transmute your lessons into power.

Karma Is the Foundation of Your Soul Contract

A soul contract mirrors the soul's highest intentions, which are not fixed. Your contract is adapted as your soul passes through lifetimes, carrying lessons from the previous life to the next. Your karmic lessons determine the basis of your soul's contract in this lifetime because the soul is not bound to repeat its lessons forever. It wants to address and integrate the karmic debts it owes, so it drafts a contract and soul plan.

The commitments between your soul and other entities (other souls, spiritual guides, or divine forces) are affected by the karmic lessons your soul carries. These commitments are how your soul creates the opportunities and circumstances to heal, grow, and reach enlightenment. It is all stipulated in your contract. You agreed to let your best friend betray you so that you could clear your karma by learning to open your heart again. It was so painful that it almost broke you, but it was co-created with the highest intention to help you fulfill your destiny.

Not every painful experience is a karmic rebalancing, and not every karmic rebalancing is a painful experience. This goes back to free will. You don't have to honor your soul contract, and other souls don't have to honor the contract they made with you. It would be nice if everything went according to plan, but that doesn't always happen.

A soul might have incarnated with the agreement to help you when you turned 28, but when the time came, they turned you away at great cost to yourself. They may have had other things to deal with, or perhaps they had a change of heart. Or maybe the timing wasn't right, and the expected support never materialized. They may incur a karmic debt or not, but the pain you went through had nothing to do with you. Sometimes, life can hand you complications that have no deeper metaphysical meaning. Sickness and accidents can cause pain without a grand "reason" behind it. The same goes for joy. Blessings don't always have to be good karma or perfectly aligned. Life is spontaneous, and while your soul contract is the path to your destiny, you must find the balance between trusting in the bigger picture and acknowledging the randomness and uncertainty of the human experience.

Types of Karmic Patterns

• Recurring types of relationships or conflicts

The déjà vu you feel when you're in another toxic relationship or having the same old argument could make you wonder if your life is on repeat. You're clearly stuck reliving the same experiences. But why? People have always said that the lessons you don't learn will never leave you alone. The recurring themes in your life aren't coincidences. They are karmic. They are the lessons your soul is trying to work through in this lifetime. All your toxic exes might be your soul needing to learn that it is okay to put yourself first. If you keep having the same fights with different people who have nothing in common, maybe it's time to look in the mirror and stop making excuses for your behavior. Your karmic debt is not punishment. Without it, you may never learn, and you risk staying stuck in the past, one lifetime after another.

• Unexplained fears, passions, or skills

Fear hardly makes sense to those who haven't felt it. You've met people with fears that make zero sense to you and them. They can't explain why they are afraid of ants or why they hate the sound of metal on metal. They'll say they were born that way. Some people were born prodigies. They have skills that people go to school for years to learn. Nobody in their known lineage ever had this skill, so where did it come from? These are signs of karmic imprints from past lives. Your irrational fear of water could be because you drowned or almost drowned in many lifetimes. You've sung well since you were 10 because you spent lifetimes honing your talent. The patterns you carry into this life, karmic or not, are your soul's attempt at healing and integrating other parts of itself. You must understand these unexplainable things about yourself to see how they fit into the larger machine that is your destiny.

- **Strong connections with certain people or places**

There's nothing like when you meet someone for the first time, and it's like you've known them forever, or when you visit a place that feels strangely familiar, even if you've never been there before. These are the signs of a karmic bond. Karmic bonds are connections from past lives that are now resurfacing to be investigated and resolved. Instant soul recognition with a stranger could be a soul contract activation between you – an agreement you made long ago to come together and work through some unfinished business. The pull you feel to a strange place might be because you have something important to learn or do there. Karma is always working in your favor; your soul knows this, and there'll be less resistance if you know it, too.

Karma, Soul Contracts, and Free Will

With all this talk about soul contracts and karma, it's fair to think you're merely along for the ride, like the universe has a plan for you, and you can't do much about it. However, you couldn't be more wrong. You are the one in charge. You're the one with the power. Your free will is your power. If karma is the structure of a house and soul contracts are its building schematics detailing the layout and function, then free will is what you do in the house. It's the color of paint you choose, the furniture you buy, and where you place said furniture. It's how you make the house a home. It's like moving into a new apartment. The foundations and blueprints were laid out before you moved in, but you get to make it your own.

The same goes for your life. Only you can interpret the role you've been tasked to play. Only you can choose what you do with the opportunities you've been given, not karma and certainly not your soul contract. You're not a spectator in your life; you are a co-creator.

If you were "destined" to have toxic, codependent relationships in this life, your free will gives you the power to recognize it, do the shadow work, and choose healthier relationships. If your soul agreed to have a neglectful or abusive parent in this lifetime, that's the karma and soul contract you're working with. How do you respond to that? Whether or not you perpetuate the cycle or heal, grow, and break free is up to you.

Your free will is how you break cycles. It is how you understand your karma, do the healing, and create a different future, not only for yourself but for future generations. You don't choose all your life's circumstances, but you do get to choose your responses.

Ways to Clear Your Karma

Now that you know the universe isn't conspiring against you, how can you regain your power, clear your karma, and co-create your life:

• Acts of kindness and compassion

Sometimes, all it takes is to be kind, not performative, surface-level kindness, but the *real thing*. There's humanity in everyone you meet, even those who rub you up the wrong way. Treating people with kindness is the barest minimum anyone deserves. So, hold the door open for a stranger, say please and thank you, and help an old man cross the street. Also, be kind to animals. Take that wounded cat to the vet, feed the neighborhood dog, or free the squirrel caught in a net. Kindness should be given freely to every living thing, including you. Be kind to yourself, love yourself, appreciate the things you've done, and celebrate how far you've come. The more kindness you give to yourself, the more you have to give to others, and the more you will receive in return. A kind word can change someone's day or, better yet, their life.

• Forgiveness

One of the most powerful ways to reclaim your power and clear your karma is to forgive. Hard as it might be, there is no need to hold onto grievances, resentments, and mistakes – yours and those of others. It's too heavy to carry through an entire lifetime, much less two. Everyone is flawed and doing their best with what they know. Forgiveness doesn't mean it didn't hurt or they didn't do anything wrong. It means you choose to drop the dead weight of anger. You elect not to let the wrong that was done to you define you. This is a gift, even if they don't know it. It is a gift that you give to them and yourself. Forgive yourself as willingly as you forgive others. Let it go and make room for love, healing, and change.

- **Conscious choice aligned with love and growth:**

It's one thing to know what you must do and another to follow through. You see a boy getting bullied. You know it's wrong, but do you speak up or stay quiet? Everyone can see that your relationship is bleeding you dry. You see it, too. Will you walk away, or will you sacrifice yourself on the altar of love repeatedly? It takes guts to make conscious, loving, growth-oriented choices that go against the grain, the hard choices. It would be so much easier to stay quiet, keep your head down, and remain stuck in the soul-sucking situation because at least it's familiar, but where's the growth in that? When you choose love and growth over fear and complacency, the universe will return the favor. What you think you'll lose by choosing growth are the anchors keeping you from reaching your highest self. Your life story unfolds with every choice. So, what will it be?

- **Taking responsibility for your life**

You and everyone else have had your fair share of hardships and heartbreaks that felt completely out of your control. However, you are not always at the mercy of your circumstances. Victim mentality is more addictive than people realize. If you allow it, it'll keep you ensnared in the same karmic patterns you're so desperately trying to transcend. You may not like the hand you've been dealt, but it is your choice what you do with it. You give away a bit of your power every time you point the finger, make excuses, or let yourself off the hook. Face your shadow and ask yourself, "What part did I play in this?" "What can I do to make it better?" This is how you choose growth over victimhood and compassion over judgment. It is how you find the light in the dark.

Past Life Regression Exercise

1. Close your eyes. Breathe in through your nose and out from your mouth. Let the tension melt away one exhale at a time.

2. In your mind's eye, see a staircase in front of you. Not just any staircase but a beautiful, winding staircase. You're at the top of this staircase.

3. Make your way down.

4. With each step, feel yourself relaxing. Let reality fade into the background as you climb down the stairs.

5. You're at the bottom now, and there's a long, poorly lit tunnel a few feet ahead. Enter the tunnel.

6. You should see many doors lining the walls. Each door is a different color and energy. Which one is calling to you? Use your intuition.

7. Walk to it and place your hand on the handle. Turn the knob and push it open. This door will take you to a different lifetime. Enter when you are ready.

8. Look around. What do you see? What do you hear? What bodily sensations do you feel? What are you wearing? Try to get a feel of who you were. Where are you? Is there anyone around you?

9. Let the details and emotions come to you naturally. Don't worry about trying to figure it out. All you need to do is be present and observant. Breathe it all in, the air, the sounds, and the emotions from that time.

10. When you're ready to leave, imagine a portal behind you. It is the door you entered to get here. Make your way back into that tunnel and close the door.

11. Climb up the staircase, and when you get to the top, open your eyes.

Affirmations

Positive affirmations are statements you repeat to yourself for yourself. They can be just the things you need when you are ill, in a dysfunctional relationship, or working through unhealthy habits, which could be manifestations of karma. Your thoughts hold so much weight. They are powerful enough to untangle you from negative karmic cycles.

Repeat these affirmations daily for 21 days and see how much power truly exists in your mind:

- I release all energies, patterns, and beliefs that no longer serve my highest good.
- I am worthy of love and abundance.
- I am surrounded by divine light and protection always.
- I forgive myself.
- My mind is clear, calm, and open to receiving guidance from my higher self.
- I trust my journey and accept all my lessons gracefully.
- I am a powerful creator.
- My body is a temple, and I treat it with love, care, and respect.
- I am connected to the universe.
- I am grateful for the blessings in my life, past, present, and future.
- I release all fear and resistance. I am limitless.
- I am a magnet for miracles, synchronicities, and joy.
- I am divinely guided at all times.

Chapter 8: Creating Your Soul Plan

Your soul plan is alive. Not in the sense that it has a physical body or a beating heart, but alive in the energetic sense. It can be updated and renegotiated as you change and your priorities shift. It communicates with you through synchronicities, intuitions, and dreams. It is responsive to your actions, thoughts, and beliefs.

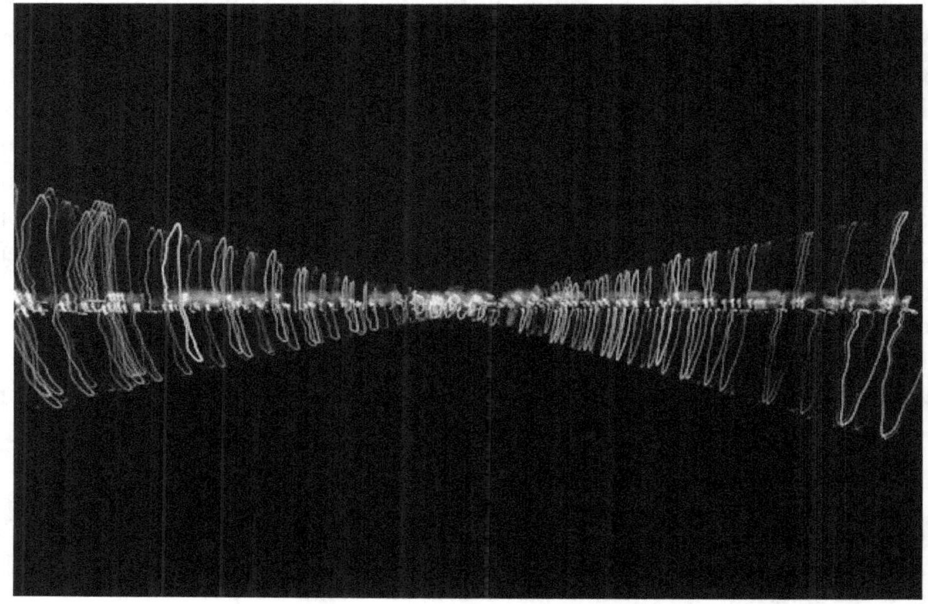

Your soul plan is already energetically alive.[20]

When you live in alignment with your highest good, your soul plan supports and amplifies the positive energies. However, when you do things that do not elevate your consciousness, your soul plan may offer you options to course-correct or to learn from the consequences of your choices. It doesn't only influence your life. It is the reason for your life.

Your pre-birth agreements are not alive in this way. They can also change, but they remain relatively the same. Your physical form is a pre-birth agreement, and so is your family lineage, your sensitivities and proclivities, your spirit guides, and your relationships. These meticulously chosen elements are based on your soul's frequency, psychic imprint, and karmic history.

Pre-birth agreements may be concluded before your birth, but your soul plan is never complete. It cannot be complete because it responds to you, and your choices dictate the route from incarnation to destiny. You and your higher self work together to direct your soul plan for your mortal life. You are responsible for how things unfold, not the other way around.

How to Shape Your Soul Plan

• Soul Contracts

The relationships in your life, intimate and casual, are not random. Your souls agreed to incarnate together in the same era, but why? What reason could you both possibly have for this? What is the purpose behind the people who enter and exit your world? These are the questions you should ask as the co-creator of your destiny. If you woke up with amnesia one day and your sister told you that you both saved $50,000 before you lost your memory, wouldn't you want to find out why? What were you saving for? When did you start saving? Where are the savings? You're not as curious about your pre-birth agreements because you don't know what to be curious about or if there's anything to be curious about. There is. Your souls chose to meet for a reason, and neither of you remembers the reason. So, half the fun is figuring it out. Here's a hint: you are here to expand your consciousness. What about your soul contract can help you achieve that? What lesson is this meant to teach you?

• Numerology

Numbers are energy. Your birth date is energy. The letters in your name are energy because they represent a number. You don't need to be a numerologist to know what the energy in a single digit says about your personality, life path, and destiny. You can do these calculations and follow the breadcrumbs your soul has left you to find your purpose.

- **Astrology**

Astrology is not only for horoscopes and fortune-telling. It offers much more than love compatibility readings. The planets exert as much influence over your life as the moon does over the ocean's tides. Natal charts are important, yes, but so are retrogrades and transits. These celestial patterns inch you closer to why you came to Earth. The skies are one of the few places with clues and assistance. Everything you see down here is a mirror of something up there.

- **Akashic Records:**

Stashed away in a library (larger than you have and will ever see) is a complete story of your soul's journey through time. Every incarnation, mistake, love story, and heartbreak is recorded with perfect accuracy in the Akashic records. It is not out of reach. Using meditation, your intuition, or working with an Akashic records reader, you can visit or call forth data from this place. There is much to learn from your previous incarnations. You have advice for your younger self, don't you? Well, what advice would you give to your next life if you could? Your answer is wisdom from only one lifetime. Imagine 50 or 1700 lifetimes. The information from these sacred records can help you make sense of your problems. It can reveal your soul's highest calling. The Akashic records contain all the answers – if you will only look.

- **Past Lives**

Your past lives are all the versions of you that incarnated for a mortal experience. Your soul is immortal and limitless, but some lessons can only be learned within the limits of a mortal life, especially a human one. The chances are, you've lived many lives before this one, and still lessons to be learned from them, or you won't need to reincarnate anymore. Figuring out the lessons is half the work, and too many people spend their entire lives not achieving them. Your past lives are a clue into the lessons you must still learn and the karma you must clear. Akashic records are a way to see into those lives. However, past life regression allows you to be in those lives. In these sessions, you get a front-row seat to life as another you in another time and place. You get to see what happened and how it could affect what is happening now.

- **Guidance from Higher Beings**

Your soul plan includes a group of higher beings that watch over you, guide, and help you. Human life is unpredictable. There are too many seen and unseen moving pieces. You may be able to maneuver the seen pieces, but what about the unseen? What about the forces beyond human comprehension? You're living a mortal life, and there is a limit to your capabilities. Beings from a higher place of consciousness don't have the same limitations, which is why you enlisted their help on your life journey. Some of these beings are always with you, protecting you and guiding your steps. Others are available to you, but only if you ask. Depending on your beliefs, you could have guardian angels, ancestors, animal guides, and many more. None of these beings, as powerful as they may be, can override your free will. So, once again, you are in charge of your life. They do what they can from the unseen world, but everything still hinges on your decisions. Meditation, journaling, and mindfulness are a few ways you can reach your spirit guides. Be open to their wisdom because they can see from much higher perspectives than you. You can co-create your soul plan, learn your lessons with them, and arrive at destiny's door already living in alignment with your highest self.

Steps to Co-create Your Soul Plan

Step 1: Reflect on Your Soul's Purpose

You'll never know what you are here to do if you never consider it. Self-reflection is the first step to understanding the meaning and lessons you're supposed to learn in this lifetime. It won't give you all the answers, but it is a solid start. Your soul knows the answers and whispers them to you constantly, except it's only loud enough when you're ready to hear them. When you're ready, you will ignore the external noise to find the internal whisper. If you're ever lost and you need clarity, ask your questions and then truly listen. You can't know yourself if you don't look at yourself. Step one to finding your purpose is getting to know yourself. What do you like? What is one thing guaranteed to make you smile? What values will you never compromise on? What do you think you do well? What is the hardest thing you've ever had to do? This is how you know the legacy you're meant to leave on the world. A curious mind will always find what they are searching for.

Step 2: Set Spiritual Intentions

Using what you learned from your self-reflection, set 4 or 5 intentions that intuitively feel right in your soul. These intentions should be themed in synchronicity with your spiritual mission.

Good examples are:

- Find ways to give back and be of service to my community
- Find healthy outlets for my difficult emotions
- Reconnect with the natural world and all living things
- Let go of my need to control everything
- Get closer to God and spirituality
- Speak the truth clearly and courageously

Your intentions will only work if they are yours. Your path is yours, and your intentions should be too. Nobody else can walk your journey for you, so it's better to set intentions that matter to you, not what you think you should want or what worked for someone else. The intentions you set today will be your light in the dark tomorrow.

Step 3: Identify Focus Areas

Focus areas include relationships, career, health, creativity, personal growth, or what feels important. Choose, at most, 3 focus areas to work on at a time. Other areas might need your attention, but these three take priority because they directly affect whether or not you live out your destiny. If learning boundaries and self-love are critical to reaching your destiny, a focus area could be self-care. You could set more intentions, do more self-reflection, or make more intentional changes in this area. The bulk of your time and attention will go into your focus areas as you work with your soul plan. Where is there a need for your attention and focus the most?

Step 4: Develop an Action Plan

Assuming you have your focus areas, next, you'll need three to five realistic actions that will move you toward your intentions.

All your actions should have three things:

1. They must be tangible. Anything too vague or open-ended won't give you clear steps to follow. Meditating more is more tangible than "being more spiritual."

2. They need to be measurable. Can you track the action's progress or not? How do you know when you've accomplished something? Meditating for 10 minutes every Thursday is much better than "meditating more."

3. They must be actionable. The steps you write down should be what you can actively do, not passive intentions. "Be more connected to nature" is passive. "Take a nature walk three times a week" is actionable.

Combined, these three elements - tangibility, measurability, and actionability - are your action plan.

Step 5: Stay Open to Guidance

Take as much help as you can get. Your mortal life is limited, even if you live to 300 years, which is a drop in the ocean compared to immortality. Your soul is immortal, but your human vessel isn't, so make the most of your time here. Your higher self and other spirit guides will send you cues, synchronicities, and opportunities that you won't see coming. Take the help. Keep an eye out for the signs; your intuition will know them when you see them. Stay open to redirections and trust that your higher self will guide you. Follow the breadcrumbs, not blindly, but follow them. Often, your job is to show up and decide - while the rest unfolds in divine timing. Trust the process; you are far from alone.

Exercise

Step 1:

Describe yourself in three sentences:

____

____

____

____

____

Which three values will you never compromise on:

____

____

____

____

____

If you could have a superpower, what would it be and why?

What is your biggest flaw?

What three bad habits do you have?

Write down five things you are afraid of:

Step 2:
Write down five intentions for this year:

Step 3:

What areas of your life need your attention the most?

____

____

____

____

____

____

Step 4:

What can you do to fulfill your intentions?

Intention 1:

____

____

____

____

____

____

Intention 2:

____

____

____

____

____

____

Intention 3:

____

____

____

____

____

____

Intention 4:

____

____

____

____

____

Intention 5:

____

____

____

____

____

Step 5:

What higher beings do you look to for guidance?

____

____

____

____

____

____

Tips for Living in Alignment with Your Soul Plan

- Begin your day with mindfulness, even for 5 minutes. Breathe and set an intention for how you want to show up that day.

- Write down 4 things you're grateful for at the end of every week.

- Schedule regular check-ins to review your intentions and action plan. Perhaps once every two weeks?

- Unplug from social media for at least 30 minutes every day.

- Move your body in ways that make you happy. Dance, do yoga, go for a run, do whatever brings you joy.

- Do something creative once every week.

- Review your calendar and schedule non-negotiable "me time." Protect this time fiercely.

- Ask yourself daily, "What's one small thing I can do today to move closer to my intentions?" Then do it.

- Keep a running list of synchronicities, signs, and intuitive messages you receive. This reinforces your trust in the process.

- Before bed, think about the highs and lows of your day. What did you learn? How can you apply this wisdom tomorrow?

- Look forward to surprise and spontaneity throughout your day. Connect with your inner child.

Conclusion

Nothing is a coincidence, not entirely. There are no isolated events in the universe. One thing has always led to another, and everyone is always where they should be. It may not be where you want to be, but that's why it is so beautifully precise. Give or take, there are eight billion people on the planet. So, eight billion soul contracts – and each is meticulously orchestrated by a greater, loving intelligence.

What about the sheer improbability of your life? From the trillions of potential sperm and egg combinations, you were the one that came to be. From the instant you were conceived, you have been guided by unseen forces that have led you to this exact moment in time. The friends you've made, the jobs you've had, the loves you've lost and found, and your body type was not a coincidence. Your soul chose this, and you, a physical embodiment of these choices, were beautifully crafted long before you were born. You are creativity made flesh.

Live your life in faith that everything is happening in perfect precision. Live in kindness because every energy you send into the universe through your choices is fed into the system to produce an effect mirroring the original choice. Live in awareness that you are a co-creator, a necessary addition to the collective consciousness. Live as powerfully as you are. There is no exact copy of you anywhere else. You matter, your choices matter, and you are here for a reason.

Part 2: Soul Trap

Your Guide to Escaping the Matrix Through Ancient Wisdom, Secret Gnostic Teachings, and Reclamation of Your Supernatural Powers

Introduction

Millions of people in their separate corners of the world are waking up to the realization that the reality everyone has been conditioned to accept is, in fact, an illusion, a Matrix of sorts designed to keep you trapped and distracted. They're starting to see that much of what they're told by governments, corporations, and the media isn't the whole truth.

There are unseen forces at work controlling your perception and the information you have access to. The comfortable, familiar world you thought was real is more or less a big screen concealing a reality more complex than the one you're used to. It is unsettling to realize how much of reality is carefully curated, but there's a bright side. If you're not limited to the world you've been told is real, it means it is possible to create something better.

Soul Trap is here to show you exactly how to do that. If you could, wouldn't you want to understand true reality and your place within it? Lucky for you, you absolutely can. This book will teach you to see through the deception and finally understand how extraordinary the human mind and spirit are.

You'll learn techniques that expand your awareness to reveal your power in totality. The unseen forces that, for lack of a better word, puppeteer the collective reality are tapped into an energy that is accessible to those who know what to do. This book can show you what to do and how to use that knowledge to manifest the life you want.

In all of human history, only a select few have understood what you're about to learn here, and they have used these secrets to achieve the most remarkable things. Some have healed seemingly incurable diseases, others have bent the laws of physics, and some have shown creativity that seems out of this world. Not one of these people was blessed with some unreachable mystical power. They were simply awake and aware in a way that most people aren't. They weren't operating under the same constraints and limitations that most people are accustomed to, and now, you are about to join their ranks.

A topic as esoteric as this deserves more than partial explanations, and that's exactly what you'll be getting. No vague platitudes, no unrealistic promises – you'll be going straight to the heart of it. So, if you're not afraid to choose the red pill and see how far the rabbit hole goes, you might as well take the plunge.

Chapter 1: Soul Trap: Understanding the Matrix of Control

A long, long time ago, there were people who lived their whole lives chained to the wall in a cave. They couldn't move their heads or turn around. All they could see was the wall in front of them. Behind them, a fire burned, and between the fire and the prisoners, there was a walkway with people carrying statues back and forth.

As people walked along the walkway, the statues they carried cast shadows on the wall in front of the prisoners. The prisoners watched these shadows and firmly believed that the shadows were all that there was. They even give names to the different shadows they saw.

The first step towards enlightenment is understanding the matrix of control.[21]

By some miracle, one of the prisoners escaped their chains. They were very confused at first and disoriented by the light of the fire behind them because they had never seen it before, but slowly, they looked around and saw the real objects shuttled to and fro by other people on the walkway. Were there other people? How did they not know this? Even worse, the shadows on the wall were not the real objects but merely a reflection.

The prisoner managed to make their way out of the cave and into the sunlight. The sunlight was so bright it was initially painful and overstimulating, but their eyes gradually adjusted, and they saw the world properly for the first time. They saw real trees, animals, and the sky – things far more alive and real than the simple shadows they had seen in the cave.

The prisoner's mind was absolutely blown, and they wanted to go back and tell the other prisoners what they had discovered. They did, but when they tried to explain the truth about reality, the other prisoners didn't believe them. In fact, the prisoners who were still chained got angry and refused to listen. They were so used to the shadows on the wall that they couldn't imagine anything else being real.

It became clear right then and there that the prisoners in the cave were trapped in their ignorance and may never be able to see the truth of the world outside. They had become so accustomed to their limited perspective that the idea of a larger, more real reality was simply too much for their minds to process.

The allegory of the cave is Plato's illustration of the human condition. Everyone is, in a sense, a prisoner in the cave of their limited understanding. They see only the shadows on the wall, the superficial appearances and illusions. Much like the prisoners, they have adapted to this narrow view and may refuse to believe that there could be anything more. Still, Plato believed that wisdom and enlightenment lie in freeing yourself from your perceptions and assumptions because they are nothing but shackles.

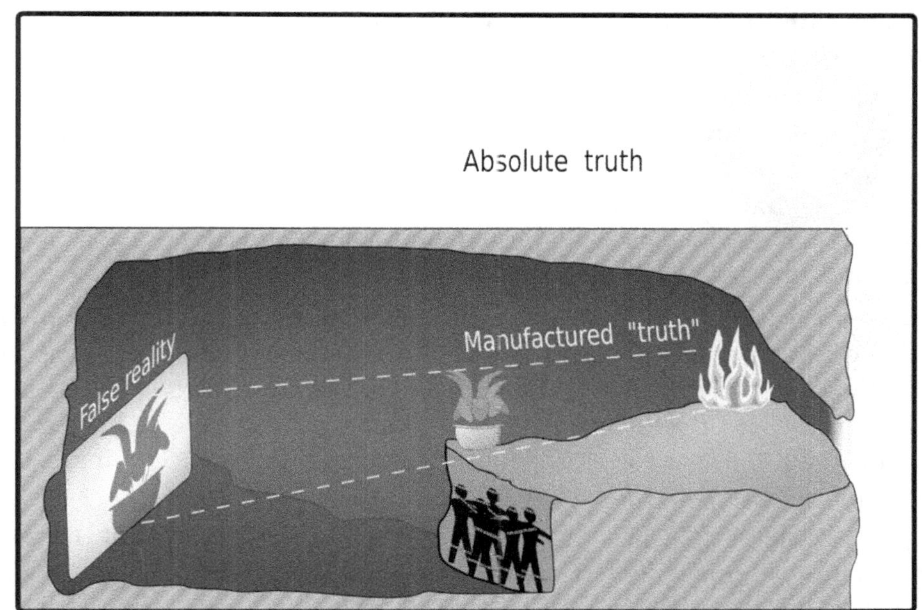

Plato's Allegory of the Cave.[22]

Much of this reality is an illusion constructed by forces you can't see to keep you obedient and docile. It's the same as the prisoners who were controlled by the shadows on the wall. The people carrying the statues on the walkway could be seen as the puppet masters of the system, manipulating the shadows and your perceptions for their own benefit. The prisoners themselves, who were content to simply accept the shadows as reality, could be seen as the compliant, unquestioning masses who are trapped within this system.

If you are to resist and dismantle the system, you need to be willing to question everything you think you know. You need to be willing to step out of the cave, even if the light – truth – is too bright and scary. Your eyes and mind will adjust because intellectual and spiritual liberation is the one true solution to the Matrix.

Soul Traps and the Matrix

A soul trap is literally that: a trap for souls. Very few souls on Earth ascend to a higher dimension after they die. Instead, they're caught in an energetic net that pulls them back into another physical incarnation. This cycle repeats lifetime after lifetime, with every soul now bound to suffer an infinite loop of birth, life, and death. You become a character stuck inside a grand simulation, unable to escape the boundaries of this material world, and the more you indulge in the distractions and attachments of the physical realm, the harder it is to escape.

The Matrix is your perception of reality. It is in no way true reality but a simulated or constructed version of it, like in the Wachowski movie, where everyone was obliviously living inside a giant computer. The world they thought they saw, heard, touched, and interacted with on a daily basis was a well-constructed illusion – a Matrix.

The way this works, according to the movie, is that your brain is connected to a massive computer system that generates all of your sensory experiences. Every single sight, sound, smell, taste, and physical sensation you perceive is created and fed to you by this advanced technological Matrix. You think you are living in the real world, but in fact, you are just consciousness confined to a simulated environment.

You could say, "That's just a movie. Movies aren't real," but the five senses are extremely limited, with a narrow and potentially distorted view of what's out there. So, what if your brain takes the information received through these senses and pieces together an interpretation, a simulation, if you will, of the world around you? Going a step further, what if that simulation is flawed or incomplete?

The Matrix is more than just science fiction. Philosophers, spiritual teachers, and esoteric traditions have proposed that perceived reality is not an objective, verifiable truth but a subjective, constructed experience generated by the mind. In Hinduism, ancient Vedic texts, for example, speak of the world as *maya* – an illusion or illusory reality. Plato's allegory of the cave also describes humans as prisoners shackled in a cave, mistaking shadows on the wall for the truth – for reality.

Modern thinkers like René Descartes, George Berkeley, and Immanuel Kant all wonder the same thing – whether the world you think you see, hear, and feel is actually an accurate representation of an external, objective reality or if it's fundamentally determined by human perception and cognition. Neuroscientists also have compelling evidence that much of what you consider to be "reality" is an internal simulation created by the brain based on sensory input that we now know is severely limited.

If reality is really only a simulation, then the term Soul Trap takes on a brand new meaning. Far from being a literal, spiritual trap, it becomes more of a psychological and existential problem for everyone.

The soul trap becomes the tendency to get so engrossed in the temporary, fleeting aspects of your life – the things you own, the roles you play, the pleasures and pains you feel. You identify so strongly with these superficial fragments of your persona that you lose touch with your soul, thereby trapping it inside a character and forgetting all about the power you have. You become so immersed in the simulation, so attached to the virtual world, that you can't see beyond it to the greater reality. This is what keeps you stuck in the birth, death, and rebirth cycle. You live, you die, and you come back to do it all again.

Origins and Purpose of the Matrix

"Red pill or blue pill?" said Morpheus. This line is up there with the most iconic and thought-provoking moments in the history of cinema, and it all goes back to the allegory of the cave. Do you stay comfortable in the familiar, even if it's a lie? Or do you take the risk if it means leaving behind everything you've ever known?

The Matrix, as Plato and Descartes explained it, is a system designed to control and keep the masses complacent and obedient. It operates through the covert manipulation sprinkled throughout everyday life. Your very thoughts, behaviors, and beliefs are manipulated to the very last detail without you even realizing it.

Plato suggested this in 360 BC when he wrote the Allegory of the Cave, and centuries later, French philosopher René Descartes built on this idea. He wondered, "How can I be sure that the world I see around me is real?" Descartes' famous line, "I think, therefore I am," questioned the basic premise of objective reality.

René Descartes.[28]

More centuries passed, and the idea of a simulated or controlled reality found its way into contemporary literature. Jorge Luis Borges, for example, wrote a short story called The Circular Ruins that featured a constructed dreamlike world where a man who created another man questions his identity and existence. Is he the creator or the creation? Is the world around him real, or is it all just a dream within a dream? Another good example is by the science fiction author Philip K. Dick, who played with similar themes in his novel The Three Stigmata of Palmer Eldritch.

The 1980s and 1990s saw an explosion in the cyberpunk genre, which made room for the overlap between technology, power, and reality. Books like William Gibson's Neuromancer and Neal Stephenson's Snow Crash imagined futuristic worlds where the line between the digital and physical spaces was blurred, foreshadowing the technologically advanced hellscape that is the Matrix.

All of these philosophical, literary, and, to an extent, religious influences came together in the genre-defining 1999 film The Matrix, directed by the Wachowski sisters. They masterfully synthesized these ideas to create a story that changed everything. The film's success and its sequels cemented the concept's place in popular culture, recasting it as a generally accepted metaphor for how human perceptions, beliefs, and behaviors are puppeteered by dark forces. The Matrix became a symbol of the never-ending fight for autonomy and the pursuit of truth in an increasingly complicated and technologically mediated world.

You are hit with mind-altering narratives, advertisements, and images left, right, and center. Your personal data is collected and shared among third-party corporations and governments, usually without your knowledge or consent. They may put out a disclaimer or give you their "terms and conditions," but how many people actually read through all that fine print? How much of the truth is even in it?

You almost can't escape it. Your phone, your computer, your streaming networks – they're all windows into this expertly manipulated reality that feeds you every bit of information designed to deceive you into compliance. It's a digital prison. You're a prisoner, and your every move is tracked and analyzed by algorithms that are more concerned with their respective agendas, which is primarily profit.

If you're not falling for the gazillion advertisements telling you that you need the latest iPhone or viral fashion item to be happy and successful, you just might fall for the news stations that sensationalize fear and division to distract you from the real issues they don't want you looking at. If you're immune to both of those, there's always social media to encourage comparison so that you're never content, forever in the rat race, and always feeling insecure.

It is cultural programming designed to perpetuate consumerism while you feed on approval from external sources. You're led to believe that the road to fulfillment is paved with material possessions, social status, and validation. And they force these ideas down your throat with a big spoonful of fear.

Fear is the most effective trick in the book to maintain the status quo and guarantee that you never question your reality. You're taught to fear the unknown, never rock the boat, obey, and never step out of line. The consequences of nonconformity are unfailingly reinforced. Nobody wants to get canceled, fired, and, in some cases, killed. You're raised to believe that the world is a dangerous and unpredictable place and that the only way to survive is to play by the rules and conform to the expectations of the powers that be. How ironic is it that this fear is nothing more than an illusion?

How Do You Get Trapped in the Matrix?

From what anyone can tell, the Matrix is the human experience, an earthly existence, so reincarnation is the biggest trap. The minute you're born into this world, you're trapped because you live, you die, and you're born again. Reincarnation is the strongest tether to the Matrix because you're unable to ascend out of this physical reality.

With each new life, you're reborn into the same limited existence to face many of the same problems as before. It matters little how much you learn or grow in one lifetime; when you die, all that knowledge and experience just gets wiped clean as you're reborn into a new body and a new persona, and the Matrix, or the forces that control it, appear to have designed this reincarnation system to their advantage. You have to believe that the cycle of birth, death, and rebirth is a natural, not to mention desirable, feature of the human experience, and there's nothing more. They know that if you genuinely believed that this earthly existence was all there was – that there was no greater reality outside the Matrix – then you'd be much less inclined to question it or try to escape. The promise of a better life in the next incarnation is nothing but a carrot dangling just out of reach.

Being born may be the biggest trap, but it is by no means the only trap. After you are born, you are mentally assaulted with societal conditioning and expectations that work to entrench you deeper into the Matrix. You're born into a world that has very specific ideas about how you should think, behave, and live your life.

It starts small – sit still, be quiet, do as you're told. Then, it escalates into more strict social rules that you're expected to uphold without question. You're taught to value the same things – material possessions, status, and productivity – over more abstract ideas like self-actualization and inner peace. And it's always for your own good. "It's important to get good grades so you can get a stable job." "You need to save up and buy a house; that's what a responsible adult does." The shackles feel like necessities, and the Matrix wins again. You're expected to have a career, get married, have children, and pretty much replicate the same patterns as everyone else in human history. Stray from this prescribed route, and you will immediately be met with confusion, disapproval, and outright rejection. Heaven forbid you see cracks in the foundation and one day question the Matrix itself. You are branded crazy and the one who is out of touch with reality. The Matrix doesn't like it when you wake up, and it will use every tool at its disposal – social pressure, fear, doubt – to pull you back in. You're living in a dream within a dream, and almost everyone has forgotten how to wake up.

Belief Systems in the Matrix

The Matrix is powered by your genuine, undivided attention, and the only way it can get it is through belief. You have to believe; you have to be fully invested, or it won't work. Belief equals trust, and up until this point, you have trusted the Matrix. It requires your trust. It's the same thing as watching a movie so good that you forget that you're just sitting in a theater. The Matrix is trying to do the same thing but on a much grander scale. It wants you to forget that the "real world" you're living in is not so real, and what better way to do this than belief systems?

They're all the same, but let's start with religion. Most faiths teach their followers that they were born flawed or sinful and that they can only find salvation in the religion's rules and teachings, but the rules must be followed strictly. One misstep and your soul is damned. The followers are then left with nothing but guilt, shame, and dependence on religious authority.

It's the same old story with science. The scientific community presents its findings as absolute facts without acknowledging that science can be biased or subjective, too. This causes blind faith in scientific dogma despite any evidence that tells a different story.

Politics works the same way. Politicians and political ideologies present their views as the only truth, conveniently forgetting to mention that politics is influenced by special interests, biases, and subjective interpretations. Opposing perspectives are sold as invalid or unpatriotic, and the result is blind loyalty to political parties and declarations, with no care in the world for evidence that may contradict the dominant narratives.

World politics are manipulated to send off specific messages to the masses.[34]

Consumerism and modern media also function as belief systems in the Matrix. Advertisements, celebrity worship, and social media condition people to trust without a doubt that happiness, satisfaction, and status can only be found in consumer culture. You are trained to believe these things because the Matrix falls apart without belief.

The mind of any conscious being can be trained or conditioned to respond in specific ways to specific stimuli. We know this thanks to Ivan Pavlov, a Russian physiologist whose work famously demonstrated how dogs could be trained to salivate at the sound of a bell, with or without food. Someone who grew up in a home where the television was always on at mealtime will most likely develop an unconscious association between eating and the TV. They may not know this until they wake up to the fact that it is almost impossible for them to enjoy a meal without having the TV on. This is how mental conditioning works. Throw in as much cognitive dissonance as possible, and you have the Matrix.

Cognitive dissonance happens anytime your beliefs and actions don't match. You could believe that you should always be honest, but then you tell a little white lie to spare someone's feelings because society says consideration is a virtue. Is that good? Is that bad? Does that make you a liar? This represents an internal conflict, the kind the mind will try to resolve by rationalizing the behavior or adjusting the belief. The Matrix feeds on this, and so you will forever be exposed to conflicting information, messages, and expectations. You're told one thing by the media, another by politicians, and yet another by religious or scientific sources, and you're expected to somehow reconcile every single one of these competing truths. No normal person can; it's too much, so their minds eventually stop trying to resolve it. It's easier to accept the contradictions and learn to live with them. The solution is a numbness to the discomfort and trust in the illusions presented by the Matrix. It knows this, and it will happily exploit your natural preference for comfort and familiarity.

Signs You're Trapped in the Matrix

1. **General Stagnation:** In the Matrix, your spark, your desire for meaning and purpose, gradually fades away. The distractions consume you to the point where any part of you that yearns for something more gets buried and neglected.

2. **Zero Critical Thinking:** The Matrix doesn't want you to question anything. It prefers if you go along with the stories and explanations they feed you because, at some point, you won't even want to think for yourself anymore.

3. **Conformity and Compliance:** The Matrix wants everyone to fit into a mold, obey the rules, and never go against the grain. The risks that come with rebellion are not a secret, and no one wants to feel left out, so they march along with everyone else.

4. **Emotional Detachment:** The Matrix encourages people to suppress or ignore their emotions – and so you feel nothing because real, messy emotions don't fit into the Matrix's tidy little boxes.

5. **Dissatisfaction:** There will always be a sense that something is missing, and it doesn't matter how much property you accumulate or how high up the social ladder you climb. The Matrix promises there is satisfaction in material wealth and status, but those things can never satisfy the soul.

Consequences of Staying Trapped in the Matrix

1. **Spiritual Atrophy:** You have the freedom to determine your beliefs, but the Matrix convinces you that you don't need to or you can't, and as a result, your connection to the divine fades into the background.

2. **Inauthentic Relationships:** There is an emphasis on superficial connections and competition in the Matrix because the system is designed to keep everyone a little bit isolated. You can't build genuine connections in isolation.

3. **Systemic Oppression:** You're not allowed to critically examine the system because the oppressive structures and inequalities that underpin society would rather continue unchecked. It may not be your intention, but your conformity is accidentally contributing to the social, economic, and political injustice you see everywhere.

Glitches in the Matrix

The Matrix isn't perfect and has glitches.[25]

The Matrix, as devious as it is, isn't perfect. There are brief but noticeable disruptions in its simulation. These disruptions are called glitches in the Matrix, and they are evidence that the Matrix's grip on you is not absolute. The cracks are your way out if you know where to look. For example:

- **Synchronicity**

Cracks in the Matrix form the weirdest coincidences. New Age spirituality calls them synchronicities. It's when two things that are so perfectly timed and connected happen that they appear to have been coordinated by the universe itself. For example, and this one has happened to so many people, you're randomly thinking about your old college roommate, whom you haven't spoken to in years, and then a few minutes later, they call you out of nowhere. One would think your thoughts somehow reached out and made them call you. Another synchronicity is seeing the same cryptic symbol or number everywhere you look and for no obvious reason too. In times like these, it's as if the usual rules that govern the world just... *glitch for a second.* Logical, linear reality goes out the window to reveal the intelligence or interconnectedness that's normally hidden from you. Synchronicities are cracks in the Matrix's programming – reminders that the world isn't robotic and there are powers and an Intelligence at work that go beyond the narrow mindset the Matrix imposes on everyone.

- **Intuitive Clarity**

When a lightbulb goes off in your head, and you just know something with total certainty, even if you can't explain how you know it, you just experienced a glitch in the Matrix. It could happen when you're trying to solve a problem that refuses to be solved, and then out of nowhere, this brilliant idea or solution pops into your head, and you don't know how, but you know it's the right answer. It makes no sense, but there it is, the answer to your problem. Or knowing what to do next, knowing the right choice, without knowing how you know. Intuitive clarity is a disruption in your thought processes, an energetic download. It is a sneak peek into Source itself and into the power of your consciousness.

- **Spiritual Awakening and Transcendence**

Spiritual awakenings expose cracks in the Matrix through transcendence. Awakenings are not a one-time thing, but there are powerful junctures in between where you transcend the illusion. This could happen during meditation or a hallucinogenic trip (not LSD; think ayahuasca or shrooms.) At these special junctures, the Matrix starts to crumble to expose a world that is much more than the limited "us vs. them" narrative that is sold as truth. You finally understand that everything is sacred and connected, that consciousness is limitless, and that there is magic in every single thing.

Traveling Beyond the Matrix

Perhaps the biggest cracks in the Matrix are the ones large enough for you to slip through to the other side – *outside* the simulation. These gateways are not just opened; they are forced open during astral projection, near-death experiences, or hallucinogenic rituals. It's hard to explain the feeling you get when you exit the Matrix. People have tried, but it's better *felt* than explained. Outside the Matrix, the separate, ego-driven self dissolves, and you merge with the universal consciousness. After that, the Matrix and all its rules and limitations appear so small and insignificant. You've touched something much more real, much more alive. The veil has been lifted, and you can never unsee it.

Anita Moorjani's life took an extraordinary turn in 2006 after she was diagnosed with terminal cancer and fell into a coma. She described leaving her physical body and floating above it. She said she felt peace and love unlike anything she had ever felt before. It was pure and unconditional love. She realized that the fears and limitations she had placed on herself were self-imposed and that she could rise above them if she wanted to. Everything changed for Anita after her NDE, and against all odds, she was later declared cancer-free. It's real, and it's all in her book "Dying to Be Me."

No, you don't have to nearly die to go beyond the Matrix. It is possible to consciously separate your soul from your physical form and travel to the astral plane – a dimension that exists parallel to this one. Your physical body is no more than an avatar that you need to exist in this physical world. Your consciousness or soul is the real you, and with the right instruction, you can detach from your avatar temporarily. Ask Robert Monroe. The Matrix is not all that is. It may seem like it, but it is only an illusion.

Quiz: Are You Stuck in the Matrix?

This quiz will reveal whether you are still trapped in the illusion or if you're already waking up. It's a simple Yes or No questionnaire.

- Does it feel like there's something off about your world – as if it's not as real as it looks?
- Do you ever get the feeling that you're being watched even when there are no cameras around?
- Have you ever questioned your memories?
- When you close your eyes, can you sense or hear things that aren't physically present?
- Have you ever had a dream that felt more real than your waking life?
- Is it normal for you to lose time daydreaming or zoning out?
- Do you get déjà vu a lot?
- Do you feel disconnected from the people that should feel familiar?
- Have you ever had an out-of-body experience?
- Do you wonder if technology and media are less for evolution and more for control?
- Would you say you intuitively understand the world more than most people?
- Do you question why things are the way they are, or do you take everything at face value?
- Were you called rebellious growing up?
- Ever had the feeling that there's something more to the world than what you can see and touch?
- Would you say the rules of this world don't quite make sense to you?

If you answered "yes" to most of these questions, it just might be a sign that you're waking up and one step closer to freedom.

Chapter 2: Lost Wisdom of the Ages: Ancient Views on the Soul

You can't understand the Matrix in totality without first understanding the soul. You can't solve a mystery when you're missing a clue. You can't have fries without dipping sauce. The whole point of the Matrix is to trick your soul. It wants to make you think that the virtual world it created is the real one and that your soul is just part of that illusion, but if you don't understand what your soul really is, how can you ever hope to deceive the deceiver?

In this chapter, you'll be taking a look at the many ways ancient thinkers and spiritual traditions have understood the soul so that you can better grasp how the Matrix is trying to manipulate and confine it.

Ancient thinkers can be the key to insight.[25]

By now, you know that the Matrix is not a 21st-century invention. You can trace it all the way back to Plato's writings, and he lived over 2,000 years ago, millennia before the Wachowskis were even born. Plato and his followers saw the soul as an immortal, immaterial essence – the true locus of human identity. They believed the soul preexisted the physical body and would continue to exist long after the body's demise, but most importantly, they saw the soul as being confined to an illusion – just like the prisoners in the cave.

Other ancient philosophers and cultures wondered the same things about reality as Plato did, as you're doing right now. Indians from over 4500 years ago, Mesoamericans, Ancient Greeks, and Ancient Egyptians all wondered if the universe was a randomly generated arrangement of separate, independent objects or if it was alive and everything was connected to everything else. They all autonomously settled on the latter.

Ancient Egyptians, for instance, had this symbol called the ouroboros – a snake eating its own tail. For them, this represented the cyclical, self-sustaining universe. They saw the cosmos as a harmonious whole, where no component was less important than the other. Hindus spoke of Brahman – the supreme, unitary reality that exists beneath and permeates all existence. From these perspectives, the diversity that has been normalized in recent centuries does not exist because we're all one. The individual self is not separate from this greater cosmic unity but is one and the same with it. This belief wasn't just philosophical to these people; it showed up in their art and architecture – the geometric patterns in Egyptian temples, mandalas in Hindu temples, and multiple pyramids in Mesoamerica.

The Ouroboros.[27]

Across these same traditions, they also believed in cycles. Time was not perceived to be a straight line with a discernible beginning and end; it moved in cycles – "birth, death, and rebirth," "spring, summer, fall, winter," "cause and effect." Egyptians had the Eternal Return, the belief that history repeats itself because the cosmos always renews itself.

The Hindus and Buddhists believed in reincarnation and the Wheel of Samsara – death and rebirth. The Mesoamericans also had fairly accurate calendar systems that detailed cosmic cycles and epochs. There was no singular, irreversible forward movement in history for them. Everything happened in cycles.

The Wheel of Samsara.[38]

Finally, they understood that the divine circulated through everything. In ancient Egypt, they believed in *"Ka,"* the life force that continued to exist after physical death. The Indians called it *"Atman"* (the true self), which was seen as inseparable from Brahman, and in Mesoamerica, the self was understood to be one with the natural world and the celestial bodies that governed them. The goal, then, was not to impose your will or to conquer the natural world. The goal was alignment with the sacred rhythms and patterns that they believed could be found in all things.

As you can see, the Matrix, the soul, consciousness – none of it is news to humanity, yet much of this knowledge somehow got buried, pushed to the margins, or hidden from the general public, either intentionally or unintentionally. Some say it was because the people in power – both religious and political – felt a threat to their authority and control, so they worked to suppress or discredit anything that didn't fit their agenda. Others blame the dominant cultural transition towards materialism and scientific reductionism in the West because it led to the dismissal of anything that couldn't be measured or quantified.

Whatever the reason, this loss is why all of this is considered New Age spirituality, but as much as this era would want to take credit for this, we just can't. What you are witnessing now is a rediscovery and resurgence of this knowledge, not its creation, but this is a good thing because it means that we don't have to start from scratch here or reinvent anything. However, if all this was common knowledge once upon a time, what happened?

Lost or Hidden Wisdom

The Library of Alexandria was the place where scholars, philosophers, and thinkers from all over the Mediterranean gathered to study, debate, and exchange ideas. It was said to have contained hundreds of thousands, if not millions, of scrolls. They said it was all the wisdom of the ancient world contained in one place. It was the internet of that time. People would come from far and wide to consult the library's collection. It had everything – astronomy, mathematics, poetry, history, etc. It had everything except a giant spirit owl. Ideas were born there, and secrets were buried there. Unfortunately, the library was burned down on purpose, not once, but multiple times, and its knowledge burned with it.

The modern view of the Great Library of Alexandria.[29]

What happened to the Library of Alexandria wasn't an isolated incident. This has happened over and over whenever those in power feel threatened by knowledge. The Gnostic Christians are a prime example. Gnostic Christians were spiritual seekers with a radically alternative belief in God, the soul, and human connection to the physical world. The mainstream Christian church didn't like that, so they persecuted the Gnostics, burned their texts, and forced their teachings into hiding.

Then there's what happened to the native traditions in Mesoamerica when the Europeans thought it was a good idea to take over. The Aztecs, Mayans, and other indigenous cultures had rich spiritual practices, sacred texts, and holy sites until the Catholic conquistadors invaded. The Europeans were determined to impose their religious beliefs and political control, no matter what. They needed power; they wanted to assert their dominance, subjugate the local populations, and force them to submit to the will of the imperial powers. So, they ruthlessly bulldozed centuries of accumulated wisdom in the name of religious conversion and political conquest.

Now, time passed, and the scientific revolution grew. Industrialization was rising, and anything spiritual or metaphysical was dismissed or devalued. Divine interconnectedness and cosmic cycles became primitive or unscientific. The world was split into chunks that could be studied and controlled. Anything that didn't fit this mold was seen as backward or unimportant. So ancient temples were destroyed, traditional rituals were outlawed, and the elders who carried the wisdom of the old ways were pushed aside, all for "progress" and a worldview that was concerned only with what could be seen, touched, and quantified. Fast forward to the 21st century, and most of that ancient knowledge is nowhere to be found.

The Soul

When you say The Soul, it sounds nebulous and elusive. What is it? Is it an ethereal, metaphysical entity separate from the physical body? Is it a poetic metaphor for the subjective human experience? What exactly did the ancients mean when they talked about the soul?

As records would have it, ancient civilizations had a surprisingly clear and consistent definition of the soul. The soul was the defining core of human existence, one that was inseparably connected to the universe itself. For the ancient Egyptians, this was the principle of Ma'at (universal truth, justice, and cosmic order). Egyptians saw the soul as the unbreakable link between a person and this universal truth. Each soul has the Ka (life force), the Ba (personality), and the Akh (spiritual self). When a person died, their soul would go on a journey through the afterlife to face trials and judgments that tested their alignment with Ma'at. If the soul was found to be true and righteous, it would be united with the divine and granted eternal paradise, but if it was lacking, it would face oblivion. A virtuous, balanced soul was the highest purpose of human life to the Egyptians.

Hindus, who have been around for at least 4000 years, call the soul Atman, and they believe it is one with the universal divine consciousness, Brahman. Their doctrines teach that the true self is not the ego or personality but this boundless, eternal Atman. However, most people live in "Maya," the illusion of separation from the divine. Spirituality is needed to transcend this Maya and achieve Moksha – liberation from the rebirth cycle and reunion with the infinite Brahman. This is in complete contradiction to the Buddhist philosophy of *Anatta*, the non-self. Buddhists don't believe in a permanent, singular soul. The self is understood to be a combination of the physical body, thoughts, emotions, and experiences. There is no absolute, eternal core. The goal for the Buddhists is Nirvana, or complete freedom from suffering and rebirth, and the only way to get here is to let go of your attachment to this fixed idea of "me" and "mine." If you accept that your thoughts, feelings, and form are fluid without clinging to them as inseparable from a solid self, you can reach Nirvana.

There were indigenous traditions as well, with sophisticated views on the soul and its place in the cosmic order. Shamanic traditions saw humanity as one with nature and the spirit realm. The soul is not separate from the body but a manifestation of the life force that animates all living things. Shamans acted as conduits, and through rituals, visions, and communion with the spirit world, they maintained harmony within their community and kept the balance between them and the natural world.

The Incas, for example, deeply respected *Pachamama*, the divine mother earth, who treated all living beings as her children. The soul, or "*Animu*," was not bound to the individual; it flowed through creation, connecting humans to the land, the plants, the animals, and the ancestors. The Lakotas and the Anishinaabe also believed in the existence of a soul/spirit. The '*wakan*' or '*manitou*' is the divine spirit that is found within all things, including rocks and rivers, birds, and four-legged animals. Humans are not separate from this; in fact, we are its caretakers, and we are responsible for harmony and balance in the natural world. So, despite their stark differences, these ancient traditions agreed on one thing: every single thing, animate and inanimate, is connected, and the soul underlines that connection.

The Hermetic Principles

This connection we speak about is literally everywhere in the universe. The planets, stars, and galaxies are all connected through gravity. Air, water, and land affect each other through their cycles. All living organisms rely on and interact with each other to sustain the biosphere. Your thoughts and actions are also connected to everyone else's. Your choices, the energy you consume, and the waste you produce are dependent on each other and everything else. These were the teachings of Hermes Trismegistus (or Thoth), an ancient sage, philosopher, and high priest. There has been a lot of debate about his existence. Some say he was a real person, while others say he was completely made up. But, real or not, Hermes' teachings have stood the test of time and are even now relevant to modern science. Science agrees that everything, starting from the smallest subatomic particles to the largest object in the solar system, is connected through elemental forces like gravity, electromagnetism, and the strong and weak nuclear forces. Hermes already said this thousands of years ago.

Hermes Trismegistus.[80]

According to him, there are seven absolute truths, now called the hermetic principles. They are:

The Principle of Mentalism: *"All is mind. The universe is mental."*

This principle states that reality is not physical; it is mental or conscious. Your mind exists in synergy with this cosmic consciousness. If anything, it is a reflection of it. Your thoughts, beliefs, and intentions are strong enough to move mountains, figuratively speaking, because the mind is the creative engine that drives the universe. Remember the quote by Descartes, "I think, therefore I am."

The Principle of Correspondence: *"As within, so without. As above, so below."*

The universe is organized in fractals where patterns or rules observed at small scales are a mirror of what is happening at larger scales. A molecule's structure is an echo of a solar system. The circumstances in your personal life reflect those happening in your family or society. Looking at a tree, you can see the same branching in its leaf's veins as you do in the arrangement of its limbs and the whole trunk and root system. This consistency is proof that there are general fundamental laws, and they replay at every scale.

The Principle of Vibration: *"Nothing rests; everything moves, everything vibrates."*

Everything is moving and oscillating at all times. The microscopic particles that make up matter are never still, even if they look like they are. Solid objects contain tiny atoms and molecules that perpetually vibrate and spin. You don't see this movement because it is happening at a lower frequency than your senses can catch, but thankfully, frequency is measurable. At a concert, when the guitarist plucks the strings, they move back and forth to make sound, but that movement is also happening at a microscopic level. The atoms and molecules that make up the string also vibrate in sync. The speed, or frequency, of those vibrations determines the pitch you hear. Earthquakes emit a low frequency, while X-rays vibrate very quickly to emit a higher frequency. All the cells in your solid human form are moving, too, down to the tiniest cell. Nothing rests; Hermes meant this literally.

The Principle of Polarity: *"Everything has two sides. Everything has its opposite pair."*

The universe functions in twos. Virtually every phenomenon, concept, or experience has its opposite. Day and night, hot and cold, pleasure and pain – these polarities are not separate; they are two sides of the same coin, connected and dependent. For every up, there is a down; for every left, a right. Good and bad, success and failure. Light cannot exist without darkness, and it is impossible to appreciate warmth without knowing cold. This principle teaches you to see the world not in black and white – but in every shade of gray in between. Neither extreme is permanent or absolute. After every peak comes a valley, and vice versa.

The Principle of Rhythm: *"Everything flows, in and out. All things rise and fall. The pendulum swings both ways."*

Nothing stays the same forever. The pendulum swinging forward will swing backward eventually. Some days, you feel enthusiastic and inspired, but other days, you'd rather curl up and take a nap. Your mood, energy levels, and your productivity naturally rise and fall. It's the same for everything – the weather, the stock market, everything. Civilizations rise and fall, companies come and go, and trends come in and out of fashion; you live, and you die. It's the natural order. It's better not to resist these cycles when you can work with them instead. No good thing lasts forever, but the hard times won't last, either.

The Principle of Cause and Effect: *"Every action has a reaction. Every cause has an effect. Everything happens according to law. Chance is but a name for law not recognized; there are many planes of causation, but nothing escapes the law."*

Nothing in this world happens in a vacuum. A thing that occurs is the result of something else that came before it, like dominoes – you push over the first one, and it sets off a chain reaction that keeps going and going. When you wake up in the morning and decide to make yourself a cup of coffee, that's an action that has a clear effect – you end up with a hot cup of coffee, but the causal chain doesn't stop there. The energy you get from that single cup is funneled straight to one area of your life or the other, leading to a chain of events in multiple directions. The mug you used to make your coffee is the effect of a cause you don't even know about. Your mom could've given it to you for Christmas after she bought it at the antique store, which bought it brand new at the yard sale of a woman whose grandfather made it himself, and the story goes on and on. On a much bigger scale, the same thing happens: galaxies collide, stars are born and die, species evolve, Benjamin Franklin is born, and you get to use a coffee maker. That is cause and effect.

The Principle of Gender: *"Gender is in everything. Everything has its masculine and feminine principles. Gender manifests on all planes."*

Opposing yet complementary forces exist at the core of everything in the universe. Everything contains masculine and feminine energies regardless of biological gender. It's the yin and yang, light and dark, active and receptive. Masculine energy is known for activity, aggression, structure, and creation. It's the protons that carry a charge and propel things forward. The feminine energy is more receptive, still, and fluid. It's the neutrons that create stability and balance. Dualities play out everywhere you look. There's action and stillness, aggression and receptivity, structure and fluidity, creation and destruction. You are not one-dimensional or rigidly defined by biological sex. You have both masculine and feminine energies. Whether or not you've integrated these two energies is a topic for another day.

Ancient wisdom might just be the antidote to society's chaos and materialism. For sure, it's on the other end of the spectrum from chasing after the next big thing, but when you think about how lost and unmoored so many people feel in this modern, extra-individualistic culture, it becomes painfully obvious that the ancients were on to something. Thousands of years later, society is the complete opposite, with all our unchecked consumption, social fragmentation, AI taking over jobs, and environmental destruction. Everything IS connected, and somewhere in history, everyone forgot, but you don't need to wait for society to catch up – to normalize what you already know is a necessity. Do your own rituals, become one with nature, and meditate more. Reconnect with your divinity, with your soul. The answers you need are hidden in plain sight, and you have as much access as the next person. The only thing holding you back is the voice in your head telling you that you're not qualified, that you have to wait for permission, that you are not worthy to touch the divine. But you already ARE divine; all you have to do is remember.

Meditation: Connect with Ancient Wisdom

- Decide on an ancient symbol you feel an intuitive connection with, then choose a place that is quiet, secluded, and comfortable.

- Light a candle or some incense to prepare yourself.

- Inhale deeply through your nose and exhale through your mouth. Do this four times.

- Close your eyes and see your chosen symbol in your mind's eye. Focus as much of your attention on it.

- While you look at it, slow your breathing so that your mind is calm and free from any distractions.

- With each inhale and exhale, sink deeper into relaxation. Let your external awareness switch from active to passive.

- Imagine that this symbol is a portal that can transport you back through time to connect you with the culture it belonged to. The symbol should glow and pulsate the more it draws you in.

- Do one more deep inhale and exhale, and walk through the portal threshold.

- Look around you. What do you see? What sounds or smells are you getting? Are you alone?

- Breathe and open your mind to energetic downloads from where you currently are. Let their wisdom pour into your awareness.

- Whenever you're ready, sever the connection and return to your current timeline.

- Open your eyes and write down any thoughts or sensations that stood out to you as you meditated.

Chapter 3: Gnostic Beliefs About the Matrix

Gnostics were one of the earliest recorded heretics, if not the first. Everything they preached directly contradicted everything mainstream Christianity stood for. Although orthodox Christianity was still in its early stages, it was on the fast track to becoming the dominant religion in the Roman Empire. The Gnostics chose esoteric knowledge over orthodox faith and doctrine, so you can see how they were a threat to Christian church leaders. The church saw the Gnostics as dangerous heretics who were misleading people away from the "true" Christian faith, but were they?

You see, Gnostics believed that this world is not the true, perfect reality that was intended by the supreme, unknowable divine force that they called the Absolute or the *Monad*. This material world you see is a flawed, limited creation brought into being by a lesser divine creature known as the Demiurge.

Gnostics believe the Absolute is the source of pure divinity.[81]

According to the Gnostics, the Absolute is a primordial, ineffable source from which pure divinity and enlightenment pour, but the Demiurge is not, and so decided to create its own kingdom, separate from the Absolute's perfection. The Demiurge fashioned an imperfect world using matter, time, and suffering. Within this world or prison, human beings ended up trapped, the soul, or "*pneuma*," obscured and weighed down by the flesh and the limited conscious mind. You, like everyone else, lost touch with your rightful nature as a fragment of the Absolute, but the Gnostics believed that the Absolute, in its infinite compassion, gifted humanity the means to rediscover the truth, and that gift is Gnosticism.

History of Gnosticism

Gnosticism first took shape as its own spiritual movement in the 1st and 2nd centuries AD, during a really important time for the development of Christianity and other ancient belief systems (like Mithraism) in the Greco-Roman era. Divine hierarchy, with the supreme God at the top, was heavily influenced by the Neoplatonist philosophers who were popular at the time. Plotinus, one of these philosophers, talked about an infinite, unknowable "One" from which everything else comes. The Gnostics adapted this model, placing the Demiurge somewhere in the middle between humanity and true divinity.

Gnostics also drew a lot from Christianity because, well, they were Christians, too. Christianity was still finding its footing around the same time as Gnosticism. There wasn't one unified, established church that determined what was correct Christianity and what was not. What they had was many movements, and people were trying to figure out for themselves what it meant to be a Christian. Some of them had ideas that were quite different from what would eventually become the mainstream, orthodox version of the religion.

For the Gnostics, their version of Christianity wasn't some heretical deviation; it was Christianity in its purest form. They saw the other emerging strands of the religion as missing the mark or straying from the authentic teachings of Christ himself. The Gnostics saw Jesus not just as a savior but as a revealer of the gnosis that could free the divine spark imprisoned within the material body.

It turns out, however, that as Christianity became more organized and centralized centuries later, the Gnostics were declared to be heretics. The church leaders who were curating the version of Christianity you're familiar with deemed Gnostic knowledge, its spiritual elitism, and detachment from the material world dangerous and unacceptable. So many Gnostic texts and teachings were destroyed, and Gnostics were forced into hiding or killed, starting with the earliest and largest Gnostic movement, the Manichaeans.

Manichaeans were followers of the prophet Mani, who lived in the 3rd to 7th centuries CE. They were persecuted and given death threats wherever they went. The Zoroastrians, who lived in Babylonia, where Manichaeism originated, executed Mani himself for his "heretical" beliefs.

Even after their leader's death, these Gnostics still had a target on their backs. Religious and political leaders from east to west issued decrees ordering the deaths of Manichaean followers on sight, but despite all odds, some of their communities held the faith, including the Bogomils, who would later birth another major Gnostic movement – the Cathars.

The Cathars lived and spent most of their time in France during the 12th to 14th centuries CE. Deciding to do things differently from the Manichaeans, the Cathars were not actively trying to convert people, but that didn't stop the French royalty and the Catholic Church from seeing them as a threat.

The Catholic Church launched a brutal military campaign against the Cathars, known as the Albigensian Crusade. During this crusade, a Cistercian abbot commander said something quite disturbing. They were about to invade a town occupied by both Orthodox Christians and Cathars, and when the soldiers asked how they would know which was which, the commander said, "Kill them all; the Lord will recognize his own." This gave the Crusaders free rein to massacre the entire town indiscriminately.

These are just a few accounts of what befell the Gnostic faith. There are many, many more. Gnosticism, at its peak, represented spiritual rebellion. They refused to be contained. They rejected the church as a construct in the Demiurge's world and all but boldly declared that the average person didn't need to rely on priests, bishops, or theologians to find salvation. They preached that God has always been within, never without, and that is why they were hunted down.

Gnostic Terminology

The Pleroma

The Pleroma is the Gnostic name for heaven – the home of the Absolute and lesser spiritual beings they call "*aeons.*" The Absolute is the supreme, unknowable divine source that remains unbound by reality in all its forms. Surrounding the Absolute are complementary aeons arranged in pairs of masculine and feminine. They spread outward from the Absolute in successive waves. The beautiful, otherworldly place is the final destination for the human soul, which the Gnostics believed had become estranged from its divine origins thanks to the Demiurge and its ignorance. The Pleroma is the source of all spiritual knowledge and power. It is home.

Aeons

Aeons are the entities that live in Pleroma. They are not separate gods per se; they are more fragments or expressions of the Absolute. You know how one person can have many qualities, talents, and roles? The Absolute is exactly like that, but in his case, his "qualities, talents, and roles" manifest as distinguishable spirits called aeons. They are separate from him and *ARE* him at the same time. These entities exist in complementary pairs, with a masculine and feminine aspect to each one. There is the aeon of Nous (the divine mind) with his counterpart Aletheia (truth) and the aeon of Logos (the divine word) with his counterpart Zoe (life). These pairings embody the synergistic relationships that exist between the two divine qualities. Sometimes, these aeons function as intermediaries between the Absolute and the material world by channeling divine energies and revelations down to the physical plane.

The Demiurge

Gnostics describe the Demiurge as a flawed or imperfect creator deity responsible for the physical world that humans live in. He is nothing like the holy, omnipotent Absolute that lives in Pleroma. The Demiurge is a subordinate, secondary deity who created the material cosmos out of pre-existing chaotic matter, and he is one hell of a craftsman. No one can argue his expertise, he did bring the physical world into existence, and it looks breathtaking, but this world does not have the wisdom and perfection of higher spiritual realms because aeons have no business creating worlds. This is the reason Gnostics believe the Demiurge is nothing but a being held captive by his own egoistic delusions and is unaware of his place in the greater cosmic order.

The universe, as you know it, is not the work of the Absolute. It was created by Sophia, another aeon who then gave birth, so to speak, to the Demiurge. Sophia, in Gnostic myths, stands for wisdom. Before the world was, she spent her days trying to know everything about the divine. She was endlessly curious, but she unintentionally created the Demiurge in her quest for more. This creation was not of love; it was a byproduct of her desire to learn more and explore, but what was done was done, and the Demiurge was born, except he was not complete. He had everything but the awareness and wisdom that Sophia possessed. He believed he was the highest power, even though he was not. He is both the creator and ruler of the material realm – the architect – but also the reason for its imperfections and limitations. He is arrogant, jealous, and resentful of the higher worlds, all of which fuel his determination to keep humanity confined to the material world. The Gnostics believe without a doubt that human ignorance, suffering, and mortality all come from the demiurge. They call him Ialdabaoth or Yaldabaoth, a half-lion, half-serpent entity who deludes humanity into worshipping him as the one true god.

Archons

The word "archon" comes from Greek and means Ruler or Authority. Gnosticism explains that archons are powerful entities created by the Demiurge for one reason only: to be gatekeepers of the physical realm. They have been described as ignorant and malevolent demons charged with maintaining control over humanity to guarantee that souls never achieve spiritual awakening. Obviously, they are not 100% effective because there have been souls who did liberate themselves, but for every soul that did, there are a million more that did not, so these archons are still very capable at their jobs. They are like the agents in the Matrix movies – almost unbeatable, relentless, and dedicated to preserving the simulation. Many Gnostic texts mention exactly seven archons, one for the sun, moon, Saturn, Venus, Mars, Mercury, and Jupiter. Some Gnostic teachings even claim that archons aren't necessarily evil; what they are is limited by their ignorance. They know nothing of the higher spiritual realities, and so they act in ignorance at the cost of humanity's spiritual freedom. Either way, they hold the gate, and they don't want you getting through.

What Is the Divine Spark?

The divine spark is the very thing that makes you human – a flame that lives in each and every one. It is a little piece of the divine consciousness, a shard that is one and the same as the infinite divine light that has been stolen and dispersed throughout the material world. This spark is your divinity. It is the YOU that is untouched by the illusions and limitations of the material world – the YOU that transcends the ego, the personality, and the physical body. It is the pure, unbounded consciousness that is your birthright as a human being. You are the divine-made flesh, and your spark is proof.

No two sparks are exactly the same – all are distinct, irreplaceable expressions of the divine. Your spark is your own; it is your signature, your soul's fingerprint. It is different from anyone else's in the world. Gnostics don't believe you need a church, priest, or holy book to reveal the divine to you. You don't need them because the divine is already inside you. Jesus said it himself. In Luke 17:21, he said, "For behold, the kingdom of God is within you."

The divine spark is what makes you human.[32]

This belief, this Gnostic truth, is both radical and natural. It's radical because it goes against the traditional structures that define religion and spirituality – a hierarchy with leaders at the top and followers at the bottom, where the "experts" are the ones who get to decide what's true. But it is also natural because it removes the barriers and filters that stand between you and the big questions you're trying to figure out about life, the universe, and your place in it. Nobody knows you better than you know yourself. Nobody is more qualified to make sense of your life and what it could mean for your soul – nobody but you. You were born spiritually intelligent, and the gnosis you need to free yourself is right there, hidden in plain sight, if you're not too distracted to see it. The Gnostics want to go home to Pleroma, where the soul belongs. Liberating the divine spark through gnosis is how they go home.

Liberation Through Gnosis

Spirituality does not happen in the mind. It is more than belief or intellectual comprehension. True spirituality is experienced and felt. It is personal, it is experimental, and the Gnostics understood this to be the only path to knowledge. This knowledge is what the ancient Greeks referred to as Gnosis. You can't learn how to swim by reading about it in a book or listening to someone explain it to you. Sure, neither of those things is completely useless because they do provide you with some information, but it doesn't compare to getting in the water yourself and attempting to swim. Gnosis requires direct experience. Like swimming, spirituality demands practice. You can read all the spiritual books you want, listen to all the lectures, and attend every workshop, but until you meet these teachings personally, they will remain abstract concepts to your soul.

Gnosis is your way out of the Matrix. It is how you break your Wheel of Samsara. Gnosis is the antithesis of blind faith. The truth is, you can't blindly obey your way to freedom. You need to engage with life. You need to feel, to explore, and to question everything. Faith in anything outside yourself gives you comfort, but it also gives away your power. The archons are counting on you to do that. Every time they see you blindly obeying a religion, a political system, or any external authority, they know they have you right where they want you. They love your blind faith because it makes you easier to manipulate and control.

Gnosis snatches that power right out of their dead grips. It pierces the veil of maya, straight through the manipulation and control tactics. You'll finally see how the archons use fear, guilt, and authority to keep humanity blind, obedient, and disempowered. And the thing is, once you see it, you can't unsee it – you can't be controlled in the same way anymore.

No, you don't need to throw away your love for religion or politics if you don't want to. You don't have to abandon everything you've believed in up until this point. Gnosis is based on free will; you get to choose, but you must be critical and selective. You can either blindly accept everything as absolute truth, or you can apply wisdom. Illusion or not, the Matrix is governed by laws and beliefs that still apply to you regardless of your belief in them. Gnosis simply asks that you carefully sift through those beliefs to keep what aligns with your evolving understanding of truth and release what doesn't. This is how you beat the archons at their own game. It is how you escape.

The Gnostic Myth of Sophia

You know, it all began with Sophia. Everything you can see, taste, and touch – the world as it is – is because of Sophia. To a degree, Sophia's story is everyone's story. It is both inspiring and a little tragic, a perfect mirror to humanity's disconnection from spirit.

Sophia was a divine entity. She still is, but in the beginning, she was a shining example of wisdom and creativity. She was the last aeon to be born in Pleroma. Her parents, a masculine-feminine pair of aeons, gave birth to her with the Absolute's blessing. She was perfect, like all the other aeons that came before her, but unlike them, Sophia wanted more. She wanted her own child, and it made her restless – restless enough to create it herself without a masculine counterpart and, most importantly,

Gnostic Sophia statue.[88]

without the Absolute's blessing. Solo creation was thought to be a violation of the natural order, so the result of Sophia's bold move was the birth of the Demiurge. This was the beginning of her fall.

Yet, realizing the gravity of her mistake, Sophia immediately tried to cast this twisted, imperfect child out of Pleroma. As soon as she did, the physical cosmos was created. She successfully banished her son to the lower, material realms, but the damage had already been done. Sophia's divine nature had been compromised by her self-directed creation, and it left her diminished and incomplete. No longer able to live in the Pleroma herself, she was forced to take up residence just outside the divine realm, alienated and fractured.

Using Sophia's power, the Demiurge – flawed and belligerent – went ahead to create the physical world and, in his delusion and arrogance, claimed it as his personal domain. He believes himself to be the supreme creator, the one true god. The Gnostics know better, though – they understand that the Demiurge is only a pretender, a poor imitation of the divine source.

He was consumed by his desire for control, so he collected divine sparks, trapped them in physical bodies, and created a system to keep them trapped. This system is the Matrix, archons, and reincarnation. It was an abomination even to Sophia, but instead of abandoning humanity, she dedicated herself to reuniting us with the Absolute. Despite her fall from grace and fragmentation, she is now humanity's anchor to Source.

Remember the story of the Garden of Eden with the serpent and strict instruction not to eat from a particular tree? According to Gnostic texts like The Hypostasis of the Archons and On the Origin of the World, both from the Nag Hammadi library, the serpent in the garden was not a deceptive agent of the devil; it was Sophia.

After the Demiurge created the physical world, he created the first humans using a combination of matter and divinity. These humans were Adam and Eve, and he placed them in a garden with one instruction only: to never eat the fruit from the Tree of Knowledge. This, the Gnostics believe, was an attempt by the Demiurge to keep humanity in ignorance, oblivious to their divinity.

Enter Sophia, the divine feminine wisdom. She appeared to Eve, another feminine, in the form of the serpent and urged her to defy the Demiurge's command. Eve listened and convinced Adam to do the same. This single act of defiance triggered an awakening that has trickled through the generations from the very first humans. To Adam and Eve, their awakening was both a blessing and a curse. Yes, they were now conscious of their predicament, but they were also still subject to the physical constraints and suffering of the Demiurge's world. He cast them out of the garden and condemned them to mortality and labor. The Demiurge was angry and thought this was a fitting punishment for his disobedient creation, but the Gnostics didn't see it that way. They believe it was a necessary step in humanity's spiritual evolution. It was not rejection or punishment; it was divine redirection. You have seen it happen time and time again. Your cousin gets fired from her old job, and two weeks later, she lands a new job with more pay and better working conditions. Or you're discarded by a narcissist, which sets you on a healing journey to integrate your shadow, and after that, you meet your soulmate. These are all examples of Sophia's redirection. She is guiding everyone, step by step, to Pleroma. She is the divine feminine, the wise one, and the keeper of the mysteries of the universe, and she will not rest until every last one of the Absolute's children is reunited with him.

The Gnostic Path

If you've noticed, Gnosticism is not everyone's cup of tea, but if you're drawn to it, you can walk the Gnostic path the same way early Christians did some 2000 years ago. It begins with:

- **Examining Your Ego and Mental Conditioning:** Without self-awareness, there isn't much you can do here. You must know yourself and observe the patterns of your ego – the false, conditioned self that you've developed based on your experiences and external expectations. The ego is always seeking validation, security, and control in the material world. See it for what it is – thoughts, beliefs, and behaviors concocted to convince you that nothing else matters but this fake, distorted reality.

- **Letting Go of Mental Illusions:** As you separate yourself from your ego and watch it like you would a puppy, you'll notice the many mental illusions and false beliefs that you've been operating under. These might be dogmas, your attachment to wealth, or a codependency on outside authorities. Ask yourself why and be willing to let them go, even if it's uncomfortable.

- **Recalling Your Personal Power:** The Gnostic path rejects the idea that salvation or enlightenment must come from outside of you. It demands that you take full responsibility for your liberation. This means refusing to abdicate your personal power to any external force, be it a religion, a spiritual teacher, or trends. Trust your intuition and have the courage to find your way home.

- **Accepting the Process of Transformation:** Nobody dismantles their ego and remains the same. You may be disoriented for a while or go into an existential crisis. This is necessary. Don't resist the uncertainty and discomfort because sometimes things need to fall apart to come together.

Meditation: Find and Awaken Your Inner Light

1. This is best done in the evening after a long day.
2. Go somewhere peaceful where you can sit or lie down comfortably and undisturbed for a few minutes.
3. Inhale deeply and exhale for three counts. Let your body relax.
4. Turn your attention inward and try to focus on the sensations in your body. Feel the weight of your body melting into the chair or mattress. Feel the gentle rise and fall of your ribcage as you breathe. Release any tension or distractions and relax.
5. Close your eyes and imagine a small, shimmering light in the center of your chest. Can you see it? That is your divine spark. It is your true self, untouched by the labels and identities you've accumulated.
6. Concentrate on this inner light, its soft flickering, its warm and steady glow. Let its presence spread within you and seep into every corner and crevice.
7. Hold this awareness and visualize the light slowly growing brighter and larger. It is pulsing, loving, and intelligent. It is you.
8. Let the light expand so much that it radiates outward to form a glowing energy field around you. This is your aura, your energetic signature, and now you can see it.
9. Bask in this feeling for a few minutes. Let it fill you with peace, clarity, and completeness.
10. Do one last deep inhale and then exhale. Open your eyes.

Chapter 4: Identifying Spiritual Traps in Your Life

What Are Spiritual Traps?

The Matrix was designed to imprison your soul, this bit, you know, but spiritual traps are not the same thing. Not really. Both slow your spiritual growth and keep you from achieving liberation, but one is intentional and purposefully malevolent, while the other... *not so much.* You'll see why in a minute, but first, are you aware that the human mind is prone to oversimplification? It loves to categorize things, people, places, and ideas into boxes. You give it a concept, and it slaps a label on it right away. This is a helpful little trick, considering you have to make sense of an enormous amount of information and sensations every single day. You take things and break them down into portions that are easy for your brain to process. It's a perfectly tidy system, but it doesn't work for everything – everything being spirituality.

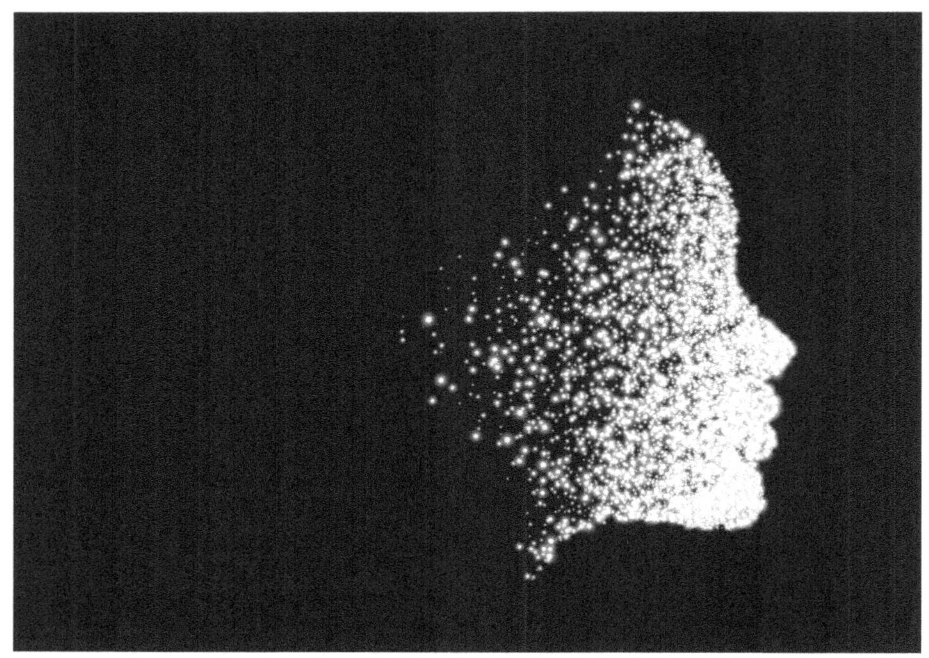

The human mind is prone to oversimplification.[34]

Spirituality has too much nuance, paradox, and layers of meaning to fit into your neat little mental boxes. Oversimplification simply won't do. It's like trying to capture the ocean in a teacup. Many spiritual people unintentionally do this as they spend so much time searching for the quickest, most profitable route to some idealized destination without realizing that spirituality is in the journey itself – the exploration, the discovery, and the potential to get wonderfully, beautifully lost. They want to rush to the finish line but fall into a trap instead.

These traps are clever and misleading. They have the most amazing camouflage, like you wouldn't believe. A good number of them are allegedly productive or righteous, or at least they should be. Take meditation, for example. Let's assume you're really into meditation and mindfulness exercises. That's great, right? You're dedicated to your spiritual growth; you take time every day to quiet your mind and connect with the universe. It sure seems like you're doing all the right things, but what happens when your meditation turns into a badge that makes you better than everyone else? What if you start thinking, "I'm so much more enlightened and evolved than the people who don't meditate"? That's not very righteous, is it?

Thoughts like these come from the ego. It's a sneaky little thing, the ego. It takes something as beautiful and profound as meditation and it twists it into a tool for self-aggrandizement. It pushes you headfirst into the spiritual trap of thinking you're superior, and it starts innocently but insidiously, like many other spiritual traps.

Spiritual traps are caused by one or more of the following:

- **Fear:** Spirituality is humanity's attempt at grasping life's mysteries. There's so much we don't understand about consciousness, the workings of the universe, and the meaning of existence. It is normal, and even expected, to be afraid of an unknown so expansive and mysterious, particularly because the mind is wired to analyze everything, to find order and certainty in the uncertain. So when you're confronted with spirituality's complexity, the natural reaction is to try and impose some structure on it. You stretch your hands to belief systems and teachings that promise definitive answers, but when you do that, it's not spirituality anymore because the definitive answers you're looking for don't exist. The answers you do receive might make you less afraid, but those answers are an understatement of the truth or not even the truth at all. It's like that old saying, "Better the devil you know than the angel you don't." You'd rather latch onto something familiar and comfortable, and that's how you fall into a spiritual trap.

- **Ignorance:** You may be born with innate spiritual understanding, but no one is born with spiritual awareness. *You have to work for that part.* Spirituality is multilayered and takes time to unravel. Everyone is doing the best they can to find meaning in it. They search for whatever models they can – ancient belief systems, New Age movements, or the latest spiritual TikTok trend – and they run with it, convinced that they've finally figured it out. The ocean will not fit into their teacup either, but they still try and maybe land themselves in a cult that advertises enlightenment, or they become obsessed with chasing signs and synchronicities instead of doing the actual inner work. None of these people are ignorant on purpose; they don't even know it's happening.

- **Ego:** Perhaps the sneakiest cause of spiritual traps is your good friend, the ego – always trying to make you feel special and better than everyone else. You might be in a better position than the next person, but that doesn't necessarily make you better than them, and there is definitely no reason to impose your perceived superiority. This is everything the ego would rather not tell you. Your approach to spirituality is not better than anyone else's; it simply is the best for you, and that's okay. No one else's is better than yours either, but if it were up to your ego, spirituality would be a competition for a prize that's not even real.

- **External Manipulation:** Throughout history, humanity has seen how institutions, especially major religious bodies, have used spiritual teachings to control people. They take these messages about the divine that should liberate you and use them to beat you into submission. Do you know how many times religions have tried to scare people into obedience by threatening them with eternal damnation if they don't follow the commandments? Or how they use the promise of salvation to compel people to give up their sovereignty and hand it over? Spiritual truths are shrunk to fit inside a box – a box that's designed to keep people dependent on the institution's authority. And it's not just them; there also seem to be darker, more unseen influences at work here – energies and entities that feed off division, fear, and ego-driven behaviors within the spiritual community. These forces don't want you to find the freedom and fulfillment that genuine spiritual practice can bring. So they mess with you and your thoughts to nudge you towards more narcissistic, power-hungry versions of spirituality. To be honest, you're only human, and sometimes you fall for it.

Types of Spiritual Traps

- **The Trap of Materialism**

The messages don't stop these days – messages that if you buy just one more thing – just get more status symbols – you'll finally be happy. The media, advertisers, and your very own social circles are reinforcing this craze that the path to contentment is littered with what you can acquire and put on display. It's such a seductive message, and it doesn't take a genius to figure out why it always works. Humans are hardwired to want security, to want community and social standing. So, when you see other people flaunting their wealth and success, it makes you want to prove your own worth and value. You automatically want to measure up. Value today is based on the properties you own, the job titles you have, and the social media likes you get. Everybody is quietly (or loudly) trying to outdo their neighbors, trying to climb higher up the ladder of material achievement, and in the process, they may lose themselves. Inner peace will never come from the next big thing. The next status symbol will not finally make you feel complete. In all honesty, people have better luck filling a black hole.

Material wealth is not evil in and of itself. Like a hammer, it's what you do with it that matters. The trap of materialism is in the relentless pursuit of more and more possessions without a care in the world for their purpose or your fulfillment. Society tells you that material success equates to personal worth, but they're lying, and if you just slow down and look around, there is nothing more obvious.

• The Trap of the False Light

Before you get into it, this is a quick disclaimer that not all spiritual teachers operate under the false light. However, discernment is a must because, in your search for spiritual liberation, you could get lured into what is called the trap of the false light. You know the type – coaches, tarot readers, or spiritual communities selling wisdom and salvation, but at their root, they are power-hungry and manipulative. They dangle a carrot in your face, but they're more interested in exploiting your vulnerabilities and keeping you dependent on them. They want you to hang onto their every word because it feeds their ego.

That spiritual coach who seems so genuine could be covertly narcissistic, and you, trying to find the light, have no clue until it's your turn to be exploited. The priest you've known since childhood could be exposed for molesting little boys. These things shouldn't happen, but they do. Anyone on a sincere spiritual journey is vulnerable; that's the truth. They long for meaning, purpose, and something more than the everyday hustle, making them more susceptible to this particular trap because it appears to be offering exactly what the heart and soul are seeking.

It's fair to want to believe so badly that you've found the secret to happiness, the shortcut to enlightenment, but these manipulative so-called experts or groups know just how to capitalize on that desperation. They'll make you feel special – like you're a member of their awakened inner circle, but beneath all that, there's nothing, no substance, no truth – nothing.

• The Trap of the Ego

Sigmund Freud, the father of psychoanalysis, made us understand that the human psyche has three main components: the id, the ego, and the superego. The id is the most primitive and instinctual component. It operates based on the pleasure principle and must have immediate gratification of its basic desires. It wants whatever it wants, whenever it wants it, and it doesn't care about rules or consequences. The superego is the moral and ethical component, the internal voice of reason that works tirelessly to vet the id's impulses and guarantees you behave acceptably. Then there's the ego, the mediator between the id and the superego. The ego's function is based on the reality principle because its job is to find a reasonable compromise between the id and superego. The ego is the conscious, rational self that deals with the external world. It makes decisions for you, solves problems, and manages your interactions. The ego is what gives you a personal identity, but as necessary as it is, it is prone to malfunctions.

Left unchecked, the ego will function like everything has to revolve around it. It will think it knows best and that its way is the only way. It will think it is better than everyone else, and because the ego defines the self, "I," you automatically adopt its feelings and beliefs as your own. You are not your ego. Anytime you say, "But they don't understand the bible like I do." That's your ego talking. It lives for validation and recognition. Falling into the ego trap means feeding your egotistical impulses, and the thing with the ego is that *it's insatiable.*

• The Fear Trap

If you've been told your whole life that if you break even one of the rules in your religion, your soul will be doomed forever, it's fair if you struggle to shake that message. Nobody wants eternal punishment or to be cast out into the darkness. Yes, you're older now, and you've sampled other forms of spirituality, or you wouldn't be here, but even if you know that those warnings are not true, the what-ifs don't just vanish. "What if they're right? What if I'm doomed to burn for all eternity?" Fear like this is paralyzing. You become too afraid, too cautious. You second-guess every decision and overthink every potential misstep. You are terrified that if you stick a single toe out of line, you're going to suffer, and it will be excruciating. Congratulations to the Matrix; their messages are working. You are frozen right where you stand, trapped.

Your spirituality is your own, and how you find God is your choice, but know this: God is love, and "love is patient, love is kind. It does not envy, it does not boast, it is not proud." 1 Corinthians 13:4. Love is absolute, and the Absolute is love. Love does not require fear; it does not demand blind submission. It is unconditional.

Is your faith love-based or fear-based? That's the question, and your answer is very important because the Matrix is counting on you to trip and fall. Living in the Matrix alone places you right at the edge, and if you don't fall, the archons will do everything in their power to shove you straight into a trap. They are always watching, waiting for their chance to feed off you, your intense emotions, especially the negative ones. When they see you teetering on the edge of freedom, their plan is to throw everything they have at you in an attempt to pull you back into the Matrix. They hack into your brain, hijack your reality, and turn it against you. You're in their world, after all, and it's an effective strategy, but the Matrix has lost before, and people have escaped. So why not you?

Signs You Could Be in a Spiritual Trap

● Repeated feelings of frustration, stagnation, or emptiness despite spiritual effort:

It is possible to give your all to your spirituality and still feel like you're not making progress. You could be stuck, frustrated, or empty inside, and it doesn't matter how many times you pray, meditate, call on your angels, or whatever your spiritual path is. This could be a sign that you're caught in a spiritual trap. Granted, spiritual growth is never a straight line – it will fluctuate, you will go through a dark night of the soul or multiple, and there may be periods where it feels like nothing is happening. But if these feelings return over and over despite trying different things, it might mean that your approach isn't what you need. You see, painkillers are good, but not when you need to treat an infection.

● Over-reliance on external validation:

Another sign you're in a spiritual trap is when you rely too much on other people, outside resources, or teachers for your spiritual progress. No doubt, guidance and contributions from your spiritual community can be the motivation you need when the going gets tough, but if you notice you are overly reliant on it, that is, you can't practice without approval, validation, or direction from the outside, there is a problem. It means you don't trust your inner wisdom and power, and so you leave it to rot while you search and search for something you already have.

- **Fear, guilt, or shame tied to spiritual beliefs or practices:**

Are you guilty, afraid, or ashamed of your beliefs? Are you afraid to practice? Are you ashamed of your faith? These are all signs of a spiritual trap. Spirituality should make you feel free and liberated, not like you're doing something wrong. If you feel anything but freedom to live your faith, then you need to ask yourself some serious questions: "Why am I afraid to live my truth?" "Are my beliefs hurting or helping me?" "Am I facing my fears, or am I avoiding them?" Your answers will determine what you do next. You need to trust that you know what to do next.

Tools for Escaping Spiritual Traps

Nobody is immune to spiritual traps. Person A may not be a victim as often as person B, but at one point or another, it has happened to everyone. You may fall, but it is up to you to stay down. You are largely responsible for your journey, and more times than you think, you do have a choice. Having said that, if you would like to avoid spiritual traps altogether or pull yourself out of one, here's what to do:

- **Practice Discernment:** Your ability to think critically and ask questions needs to be sharp as a blade. There are very few things more important. Don't blindly believe everything you're taught or told, whether it feels right or not. If it feels right, ask yourself why. Why are you drawn to a specific faith? Why would you rather do this instead of that? If it feels wrong, ask why. Why does it make you uncomfortable? Why do you not agree? You'll be much harder to fool if you don't take everything at face value.

- **Do Shadow Work:** Shadow work is any practice that confronts and heals your shadow. Your shadow is anything about yourself you'd rather keep in the dark, intentionally or not. Shadows could be secrets, shame, trauma, sexual orientation, etc. You need to confront this side of you before you can free yourself from the unhealthy patterns that could land you in a spiritual trap. If you are whole and integrated, not halfway in the dark, these traps may not appeal to you as much.

- **Trust Your Inner Authority:** You have wisdom right there in your soul, and it is meant to guide you when you need it to, but when you keep looking to everyone else for answers, you disregard what your soul has to say. And most times, your soul warns you before you fall into a trap, but you're not listening. There has to be a revival of the connection between you and your divine spark. Shamans, teachers, spiritual leaders, or anything outside yourself can not hold a candle to the flame that is your soul. That flames hold the truth, and the truth is that salvation comes from within. This inner authority helps you walk your spiritual path with confidence, authenticity, and a direct purpose.

- **Rebalance Your Mind, Body, and Spirit:** Your spirituality should be obvious in how you live your life. Don't forget that spirituality demands practice. You can pray 100 times a day, but if you can't take care of the one vessel you have been entrusted with, what's the point, you know? Your mind, body, and spirit are connected in ways you can't begin to comprehend. You shouldn't neglect one in favor of what you think the most important one is. They're all important, so meditate as much as you exercise. Eat healthy as much as you say your affirmations. Embody your spiritual growth so that your inner and outer worlds move in sync.

- **Be Aware of Energy Dynamics:** Self-awareness is one thing, and environmental awareness is another. The people, environments, and information you expose yourself to affect your energy overtly or covertly. Some add to your energy, while others drain it. You must know which things drain your energy and cut your exposure to them. This could mean setting boundaries, cleansing your energy field, or just being more discerning about where you invest your time and attention. Distractions are everywhere, and they're all competing for your energy. Energy is currency, including yours. Don't just give it away.

Clearing Meditation

1. Settle into a comfortable position either on the floor or in a chair.

2. Breathe in deeply and slowly through your nose, then exhale through your mouth. Do this four times or more until your body relaxes.

3. Close your eyes, tune out the outside world, and go inward. Try to feel the sensations in your body.

4. Scan your body and see if you notice any tight, tense, or blocked areas. Let your intuition guide you to the blockage and allow the sensation to flow into your awareness.

5. Wherever you feel stuck or stagnant energy, concentrate your attention there. Don't force it, be gentle.

6. Continue breathing deeply and imagine that with each inhale, you're drawing fresh, calming energy into those blocked areas. This fresh energy is warm and soft. Let it flow in and fill up the spaces that feel restricted.

7. Then, on the exhale, imagine the tension, heaviness, or negativity flowing out as the soft energy takes up more room. Imagine it to be a thick fog leaving your body and dissolving into nothing.

8. Continue breathing like this. Inhale the healing energy and exhale the fog. If you're doing it right, you won't have to force anything. You only need to be present.

9. After a few minutes at this, you should feel the blocked areas soften and open up. If you don't feel it yet, continue breathing into them with intention.

10. Throughout this process, be kind and patient with yourself. Trust that your body knows exactly what it needs to let go of to be balanced and free.

11. At the end of your session, slowly reconnect with your surroundings and open your eyes.

Shamanic Journey Visualization

1. Sit down or lie down.

2. Take three deep breaths and close your eyes.

3. See yourself descending down a pathway. It is a bit steep, but you're managing just fine. Take your time. The path is rich with dark soil and moss, winding through trees that look 1,000 years old. The more you descend, the softer the light grows. The air is cooler here, and it smells *earthy*.

4. Continue down the path until you reach a cave entrance with a giant boulder for a door. This is your lower world, and it can look like whatever you want it to look like.

5. When you're ready to go in, imagine the boulder rolling away from the entrance.

6. Step into the cave. The air here has a slight dampness to it.

7. The deeper into the cave you go, the smoother the walls become. Run your palm across the wall. Feel how smooth it is.

8. The cave should open into a large chamber. Walk into this chamber.

9. Walk to the center of the chamber. Your spirit guide will be waiting for you. Acknowledge their presence and thank them for coming here to be with you.

10. If you have questions, now is the time to ask.

11. Your spirit guide will do a quick scan of your energy and body now. Let them. They are searching for the areas that are heavy and blocked. Do you have any emotions or sensations that need to be released? Bring your awareness to these areas and visualize a bright light radiating from your spirit guide's heart space. Watch it as it pulses and penetrates your body to cleanse any toxicity and stagnation.

12. As the light moves through you, welcome the release, the letting go, the cleansing and purification that is taking place.

13. When it is complete, and you'll know when it is, thank your spirit guide and say goodbye.

14. Leave the cave and slowly make your way back up the path. When you reach the very top where you began, open your eyes.

Chapter 5: Adhering to Your Soul Contract and Purpose

Believers in predestination say that your life is scripted and everything that happens to you is due to a larger, divine plan. Libertarians, those who believe in free will, say the complete opposite: you are not bound by a pre-written script, and you have the autonomy to decide your fate. This debate between predestination and free will has been raging since humans knew how to write, and there have been fair arguments on both sides, but what about a third side? One that exists somewhere in the middle.

The debate between predestination and free will has been in the works for ages.[35]

A soul contract is a combination of predestination and free will. You may or may not have heard of this before, but there is a belief that every soul is incarnated with a plan, a sort of rough sketch of how their human life would go. Your soul did this, too, before incarnating into the physical world. You made an agreement or contract detailing the key experiences, relationships, and lessons you would encounter in this lifetime.

This contract is not rigid, but you can't exactly avoid it either. It is one part predestination in the sense that you have to get from point A to point B; that's the plan, but you have free will because how you go from point A to B is your choice.

The main junctures in this plan – the unavoidable incidents, relationships, and lessons – have already been agreed upon by your soul, and for a good reason. That breakup? Your rough childhood? Marrying your best friend? That eye-opening conversation you had about spirituality at 22? These are all likely pre-incarnational agreements. It doesn't make the painful ones any less painful in the moment, but there's a lesson somewhere in there that your soul decided would be best learned this way.

Saying "a" soul contract is actually somewhat misleading because it suggests that it is one soul per contract when, in truth, one soul could have multiple contracts. You could have one around relationships involving the people you're meant to connect with, for example, your life partner, close friends, perhaps even toxic family members. The karmic ties and lessons you set to learn through these relationships are written in this particular contract. Your soul could also have a contract around work and purpose. This one will specify your favorite activities, your career trajectory, and the service you'd be drawn to in this lifetime. You might also have a soul contract around your health or your creativity, financial abundance, and maybe your role as a parent.

Interestingly enough, these soul contracts don't operate in isolation. They're all intertwined, influencing and informing one another as your life plays out. Your relationships could affect your health. Your health could lead to your creative breakthrough. Your financial abundance (or lack thereof) could affect your career trajectory. Anything can happen. You're not looking at one single plan; it is a symphony, one that was written long before you could even breathe air.

In Matrix: Reloaded, if you've seen the Matrix movies, Neo was caught between two choices. He could either save Trinity or save Zion. He had to choose between love and duty, but the oracle said to him, "You didn't come here to make a choice. You've already made it. You're here to understand why you made it." Of course, you have free will, but like Neo, you're also not here to agonize over what the right choice is. You're here to trust that your soul has placed you exactly where you need to be for reasons that are for your highest good. 9 times out of 10, you absolutely need to trust the process.

The Purpose of Soul Contracts

The primary purpose of soul contracts is spiritual growth and evolution. Metaphysically speaking, the reason you even incarnate into physical human form in the first place is to have experiences that create an environment for your soul to learn, expand, and finally return to wholeness and unity with the divine.

You are a spiritual being having a human experience. Your soul comes from a higher, non-physical dimension, but you chose to visit Earth and live as a physical, embodied being for a time. This physical incarnation is a school of sorts for souls, a chance for you to grow and evolve in ways that wouldn't be possible if you remained in the spiritual realm. You've been to school, and you know how it goes – you'll take tests and be tempted, you'll make mistakes, and sometimes, you'll fail, but at the same time, you're learning what to do and what not to do. You're growing and becoming wiser. You know your story, but do you see the lessons from high school? Unforgettable. And you probably hated high school. It's the same with an earthly incarnation. You hate it, then you love it, then you hate it again, but through all that, you're always growing.

Dolores Cannon, author and one of the most popular hypnotherapists in human history, spent more than 40 years studying soul contracts through her work with past-life regression. While she lived, she maintained that nothing in life is accidental. She believed that every event, every relationship, and every test you're faced with in this lifetime is written in a carefully drafted soul contract that you designed before incarnating. From her research, she concluded that the soul is far wiser and more thorough than the conscious, physical self can ever fathom. The forethought and planning alone that go into arranging the events in a human life in perfect order is dizzying to think about.

Your soul anticipated your needs with unimaginable precision. Your contract is not a copy of anyone else's. Your lives could look similar to a degree, but no two contracts are exactly the same. You could be here to learn the same lesson, but your soul's ideas for how that should happen are completely different. Your soul knows what you need before you even know you need it, and a lot of the time, what you'd prefer and what you need are two different things.

Assuming there's a disability clause in your soul contract, it's understandable to feel anger or go as far as wishing you were never born, but what if your soul knew that this would be the most effective way to teach you patience, humility, and unshakable strength? Disability is a sensitive subject because no one in their right mind would choose to live such a difficult life, and then you tell them that their soul chose this? "How dare you?" is the response you'll probably get, and that is valid. It's not easy to see past immediate suffering. For some people, it's damn near impossible, but what if there truly is a method to this madness?

You don't have to believe in soul contracts to find the purpose in your pain or the lessons in your frustration. The lessons are there regardless; it's only a matter of perspective. You can believe your soul chose this or not, but your life has meaning, and your experiences have a purpose. Your suffering is real and valid, but maybe, just maybe, there is a reason beyond what you can see.

It's the same with other soul contracts you may have, the nice ones and the not-so-nice ones. Unfortunately, the quickest way to learn is often the hardest, and Earth is rife with opportunities for hardship, but if you can find the WHY, no matter the experience, you're already halfway done.

Free Will in Your Soul Contract

A soul contract does not negate your free will. What it does is provide a structure within which you can exercise said free will. There may be a predetermined plan, but you can still make your own choices and decisions inside that larger context. Your soul contract is there to establish the general themes, relationships, and growth opportunities you'll come across, but how you respond to those opportunities is up to you. If you're face-to-face with a problem, you can lead with courage and wisdom, or you can let fear take over and avoid the problem altogether. You can commit to healthy connections, or you can sabotage them all by yourself. They say you can take a horse to the river, but you can't force it to drink.

The best part is that because you have free will, there's not one right path you have to follow. There are countless possible directions your life could take. Your soul may have envisioned an optimal route for your growth, but you're not limited to that. Every choice you make, every fork in the road you meet, has the potential to shift your trajectory in unpredictable ways that could shock even your soul.

Along with free will comes a plethora of choices.[86]

Your choices matter, but that also means you have to take responsibility for those choices. You can't blame fate or say, "It's that stupid soul contract," when things don't go how you want them to. Your choices have real consequences, positive and negative, contract or not. You can choose to drive carefully, stay in your lane, and arrive at your destination safely. Or you can go 80 on a 50, swerve all over the road, and risk crashing. It really is your choice.

That's not to say that everything will always go exactly as it should, even if you do make seemingly good choices. Life is fickle, and sometimes, there will be circumstances that are out of your control. What if a soul you have a pre-incarnational agreement with doesn't fulfill their end of the bargain for whatever reason? What about soul connections that turn karmic because someone made a different choice? Does that mean everything is ruined? Absolutely not. You need to have faith in your soul and its ability to course correct. Soul contracts are flexible, and you are always where you should be.

The Connection Between Your Soul Purpose and Liberation from the Matrix

The end goal for every soul incarnating to live a human life is to return to and merge with Source. As you may have noticed, this is harder than it looks, and it looks rather hard. Between soul lessons, the Matrix, and the energetic parasites called archons, there's quite a bit of debris separating you from Source. The lessons you incarnated to learn are hard enough without having to escape an obstacle course that wants nothing more than for you to stay. In fact, half the work is figuring out what the lessons are, and some experiences are repetitive, so you'll think you learned THE lesson, but you probably only learned A lesson. Well, here is a secret for you: the more you live in alignment with your soul purpose, the less you have to worry about the Matrix.

The Matrix knows that you are here for a reason and that when you achieve what you came for, you won't need to be here anymore, and it knows it can't outrightly force you to be here because you're too powerful. Why do you think it resorts to deception, manipulation, and other tricks? It needs you to *want to be here.* When you die, it lures you back in with whatever it thinks will work: fear, love, family, riches, etc. If it works, you draft another soul contract and reincarnate because you clearly could use more lessons. Then you go on to live another human life with the Matrix filling your mind with worries about not having enough, not being good enough, and not being safe.

If you know why you're here and what you're meant to be doing, or if you're at least trying to figure it out, you're not going to be as easily swayed by false promises and illusions. You'll be bombarded with signs and synchronicities from the divine, confirming that you're on the right path. Your light will illuminate your life, leaving little room for the shadow to take hold.

Life doesn't automatically become perfect or 100% smooth sailing after realignment. You still have soul lessons to learn, and the Matrix is always there, waiting to catch you off guard, but there will be a palpable difference in how it responds to you and your power. Your very presence will be a lighthouse to others who also want to walk the divine path. They'll see the light in you and be drawn to it, hoping to find faith and motivation in your example. Living in alignment with your soul purpose is your ticket to freedom.

Signs and Symptoms of Misalignment

- **Persistent Dissatisfaction:** If you always get the feeling that something is missing, no matter what you achieve or own, you may not be living in alignment with your purpose. This could manifest as comparison and always scrambling to catch the next wave but never being quite happy or satisfied. Your discontent is your soul attempting to course-correct.

- **Repetitive Problems:** Some people are always fighting the same battles, learning the same lessons, dealing with the same negative issues, and entering the exact unhealthy relationships over and over again. If you're one of these people, your recurring patterns are hints pointing you back to the lessons you keep missing. The first time is difficult, the second time is also difficult, but the third time? That's when it gets annoying, and you're bound to get frustrated, but instead of frustration, how about curiosity? Going over these recurring themes can show you the areas of your life that require more of your attention and effort.

- **Feeling Lost:** Disconnection from your soul purpose comes with confusion and uncertainty. You're not sure what direction you should be heading because you have no idea where you're going. Asking yourself, "What am I doing with my life?" or "Is this all there is?" multiple times a week is a sign that you feel lost. Feeling lost and being lost are two different things, mind you. You are always where you should be, but it helps you if you have a strategic focus. So next time you feel lost, take it as a sign to stop fighting life, look inward, and realign with your soul.

Disconnecting from your soul purpose can leave you feeling lost.[37]

- **Physical and Emotional Issues:** Your body and emotions reflect the relationship you have with your soul. It's not unheard of for misalignment to come with physical symptoms like fatigue, unexplained body aches, or a weakened immune system. Emotionally, you might be more anxious, depressed, or generally disconnected from your feelings. Imbalances always call for a rebalancing. Your soul could be trying to let you know that something energetic is wrong.

How to Recognize Your Soul's Guidance

- **Meditation**

Meditation is an age-old method for temporarily disconnecting from the physical world to connect with your soul or the universe. If you can take a few minutes to shut off the chatter in your mind, you create space for your soul to speak, and not necessarily in the literal sense. You may or may not hear a voice, but you might get a feeling instead, images, or intuitive downloads. Regular meditation teaches you to recognize your soul's voice. 5 or 10 minutes a day is enough. You don't have to do anything elaborate if you don't want to. You can keep it simple with breathing exercises, affirmations, or good old visualization. Trust yourself and trust the process.

Meditation is an age-old method.[88]

• Journaling

Writing in a journal can grant you access to your soul's guidance when you need it most. Writing helps you process your thoughts and feelings. It helps you detangle your experiences and find patterns within them that you wouldn't have noticed otherwise. Sometimes, your hands might be moving across the page, but it's not your words, or at least not your ego's words. It's your higher self. Your hands are the tool, and the journal is a conduit. Pick up a notebook one day and just write. Write freely without worrying about how it sounds or looks. Write even if it doesn't make sense. Things of the spirit hardly make sense to the mind, and that's why you have faith.

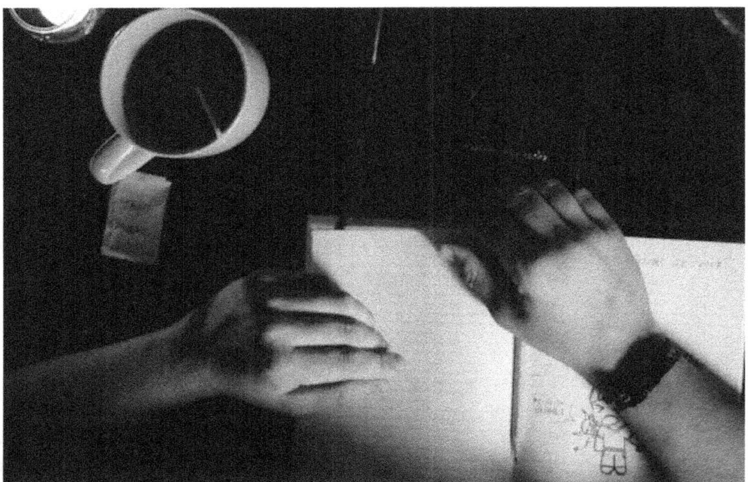

Access the deepest parts of your soul through journaling.[89]

• Intuitive Practices:

You have a sixth sense that is no less powerful than those tarot readers you go to or that preacher you depend on. The difference between you and them is theirs has been developed and refined through dedicated practice and experience. Some people naturally have the gift, but everyone is capable. Everyone has intuition because that is the strongest connection you have to your soul. The way intuition works is that you just know without knowing how you know. The problem then becomes trusting what you know. It's hard because the mind is a logical beast with very strict rules and the backing of society. Society says logic is "facts," while intuition is unreliable. That's calling the soul unreliable, and if you're taught to doubt your soul, you'd be less inclined to connect with it and less likely to live in alignment with your purpose. Do you see where this is headed?

Intuition is the soul's first mode of communication, and so long as you have a soul, your intuition can be strengthened, so buy your own tarot deck, get a pendulum, and put your intuition to the test as often as possible. Practice makes perfect.

You can put your intuition to the test using a pendulum.[40]

Meditation: Recall Your Soul Contract

1. Sit down or lie down somewhere quiet and peaceful.

2. Do three deep inhales and exhales, then close your eyes.

3. Imagine you are standing in the middle of a peaceful meadow. The sun is shining, the birds are singing, and you feel a soft breeze caressing your skin.

4. Look around to find a path that leads into a thick forest. You're not afraid. Intuitively, you know this is the way to the Akashic Records – the energetic library that contains every story, lesson, and soul journey of every soul to ever exist.

5. Walk down this path excited and curious about what you might discover.

6. You'll get to a point where the trees part, and in front of you is the tallest ancient building you've ever seen. You can feel the energy of this place in your bones.

7. There are steps leading to a door. Climb the steps and enter the building.

8. Immediately you enter, there is a desk unlike any design you've ever seen before, and behind it sits an entity. This will be your personal guide through the Akashic Records.

9. This guide greets you kindly and acknowledges your desire to connect with your soul contract.

10. They then invite you to ask any questions you may have.

11. Before you fire your questions, breathe and relax. Open your mind to receive the answers.

12. Now, ask your questions.

13. You may receive images, hear messages, or have an epiphany. Don't rush through this part; let the information flow in and out of your awareness as it pleases.

14. If it feels like you have received all the information you were given, breathe and sit with this feeling.

15. When you are ready to leave, thank your guide and make your way out of the building.

16. Once you're outside, gently reconnect with your physical body and bring your awareness back to your immediate surroundings.

17. Open your eyes.

How to Break Free from Disempowering Beliefs

- **Cultivate Self-Trust:** Add regular self-reflection to your routine, either through meditation, journaling, or simple introspection. Get to know your soul, and learn to trust it. When you need to make a decision or find your way out of a sticky situation, check in with your intuition. What is it telling you? Don't always defer to what other people think you should do; take 10 minutes and ask yourself what you think you should do. This way, you make choices that are in line with your values and highest good.

- **Question Your Conditioning:** As an adult, it's about time you examine the beliefs, habits, and thought patterns that you've picked up from your environment. It's nothing to be ashamed of. Everyone is prone to internalizing messages and opinions from the collective. The only problem is that these messages don't always resonate with who you are or what you value, and it doesn't even mean that the message itself is bad. It simply isn't for you. So ask yourself, "Where do my beliefs come from? Do they feel authentically mine, or are they things I've been told I should believe?" Ask these questions every time there is a collective narrative that you're expected to accept. Your soul knows the answer.

- **Establish Energetic Boundaries:** Be selective with the energy you permit into your life from social media, the news, and also people. Watch how you feel after you engage with these people or places. Are you energized and inspired or drained and discouraged? There isn't a single thing wrong with being selective about what you expose yourself to. Your peace is yours to protect, and it is your right to curate your environment however it best supports your growth.

- **Reclaim Your Sovereignty:** There's only so much blame you can put elsewhere before you're forced to take accountability. As far as life goes, you have power, real power. Life may be chaotic, but how do you make the best of the choices you have? How do you show up for yourself? The easier thing to do is be a victim and affirm that you have no say in what happens, but you didn't choose a human life to go where the wind blows. You're always making a choice, whether or not you think you are. So why not make it intentionally and BE a co-creator?

Tips for Living in Alignment with Your Soul

- Begin your day with a grounding exercise. If you can, place your bare feet on the ground for a few minutes to connect with the earth.

- Write down five things you're grateful for at the end of every day.

- Set a soulful intention for the day. Ask, "How can I make a positive difference today?" and do just that.

- Physical activity is a reminder that you're alive. Add exercise to your weekly routine, such as yoga, long walks, or dancing if you like to dance.

- Spend time outside. Appreciate the beauty around you.

- Self-care rituals feel nice regardless of gender. So, make time for yourself to indulge in a self-care routine that feels good for you.

- Limit your screen time.

- Drink water and eat wholesome foods, not junk food every day.

- You don't need to be an artist to express yourself creatively. Art is cathartic, and that could be just the thing you need.

- Spend more time with the people in your life who make you feel great.

- Review your priority list and see if it needs to be rearranged.

- Take breaks throughout your day to unplug and recharge.

- Say thank you often or express your gratitude through thoughtful actions.

- Do at least one kind deed every day.

- Communicate with the divine however you prefer. You could pray, perform a ritual, or perhaps speak directly to the divine.

- Trust that your soul's journey is unfolding in perfect timing.

Soul Purpose Statement

This exercise is a mix of journaling and affirmations. You're going to write down what you believe in, what you stand for, and what you think your mission in this lifetime is. Your current reality doesn't have to reflect this mission yet, but you know in your soul that this is what you came here to do. Affirm it and write it down below.

____

____

____

____

____

____

____

____

Chapter 6: Activating Your Supernatural Gifts

The X-Men movies shook the world every time a new one was released. The first one came out and had the world in shambles because no one had EVER seen anything like that before on the big screen. You had mutants prancing about with powers that shattered the laws of nature, or at least what we think the laws are. For that reason, cool as they were, all mutants were treated as dangerous and unnatural – something to be feared and contained. X-Men may have been an exaggeration of superhuman gifts, but there ARE "mutants" in the real world, you know. In many ways, you're a mutant. So is your neighbor, your friend, and your family members. In fact, if they have a soul, they are mutants.

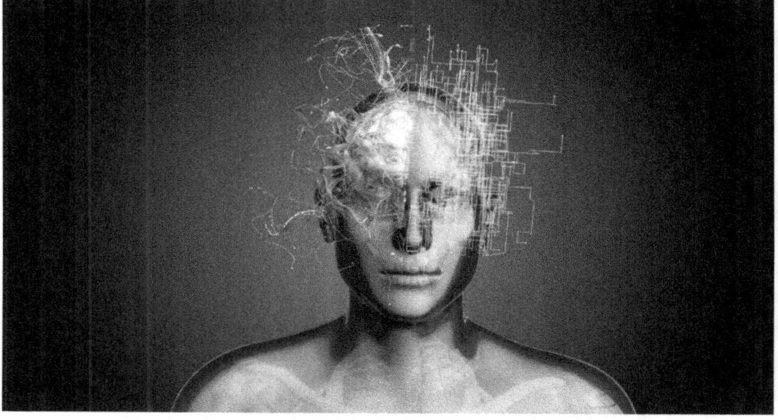

Tap into your supernatural gifts."

Supernatural gifts are any abilities that bypass the 3D and grant a person access to dimensions of consciousness, energy, and perception that are not normally available to the average person. These gifts are sometimes referred to as extrasensory because they depend on senses that extend past the standard five physical senses.

Right now, you may be skeptical about believing you have supernatural gifts, but that is only because yours are largely underdeveloped. If you're more intuitive than the average person, you may have noticed a few glitches here and there but were never quite sure because these things only happen in movies, right?

You see, your gifts are like muscles you've never used. You have them, but they're so weak you might not even know they're there. A big reason for this is societal conditioning. From as young as 4 years old, you're taught to trust only logic, reason, and the five senses. There's a strong emphasis on the material world, on what you can see, touch, and measure. Anything that can't be explained by science is dismissed as imagination or coincidence. You're subtly (and not so subtly sometimes) discouraged from anything to do with intuition and the unseen.

Then there's fear. The average person is afraid of what they don't understand. The mere thought of having supernatural abilities can be scary, especially if you were raised to see such things as demonic or dangerous. You could worry that people will judge you, mock you, or cast you out if you dare speak up about your paranormal experiences or damn-near accurate intuitive hits. To be fair, judging by humanity's response to the incomprehensible so far, they just might. So, out of fear and common sense, you bury your gifts so far down the tube and pretend they don't exist. It's easier and safer to conform and fit in than to risk being seen as weird or "crazy."

Now, to the final, if not most important, reason for this supernatural dormancy, you have the disconnect that currently exists between people and their divine essence. This is the modern era. Everyone is too busy, extremely stressed, and very detached from themselves that they forget the connection was ever there. Hours on hours are spent scrolling through social media, people are working even longer hours, and everyone is chasing after wealth so intensely that there is little time left for introspection, not to mention meditation. When you're disconnected from your inner self, there is no way you remain connected to your intuition, your empathy, and your other gifts. One cannot exist without the other.

Types of Supernatural Gifts

- **Intuition**

If you've ever been driving through a new city and your GPS malfunctions all of a sudden, this may have happened to you at least once. So, you've never been here before, and you definitely don't know where you're going, but you have an odd feeling that you should turn right at the next intersection. You can't explain it; you haven't seen any signs, and the GPS (before you lost the signal) told you to keep heading straight – but you just know that turning right is what you should do. So, you turn right, and suddenly, the signal comes back, and you're actually right on track. That's the definition of intuition. Intuition is that inner voice, that gut feeling, that knowing that guides you when there's no explanation or when the explanation doesn't make any sense. It is more than a hunch; it's a knowing that comes from a place the conscious mind can not comprehend. It is a power only the soul can give. When people say "Trust yourself," they mean trust your intuition. Generally speaking, it is the easiest supernatural gift to unlock – that is, compared to the others.

- **Empathy**

A movie that makes you cry is proof that you have empathy because why else would you cry unless your empathy puts you right in the character's shoes? Why would you cry unless you felt their pain as if it were your own? Your empathy is the reason you understand and share other people's feelings. It's the reason you are able to suspend your biases and see the world through their eyes. Empathy goes further than feeling sorry for somebody; you literally feel what they feel. You know where it hurts and how it hurts. It might shock you to know that not everyone has empathy. They can't tell when a person is sad, angry, or hurt, which sometimes translates into not caring. They can see the sadness if it is outwardly displayed or expressed, but they can't feel the sadness themselves.

Now, among the people who do have empathy, there are a select few within that group called empaths. Empaths can sense the emotions of the people and spaces around them, including when those emotions are intentionally hidden. They walk into a room and absorb emotions like a sponge; they can't help it. It might help with their discernment, but it doesn't always feel like a gift. Some empaths can't tell where their emotions end and others' begin. They feel everything, and they don't have to know you to pick up on your emotional state. Empathy is a gift, though. It makes you a better friend, partner, and human being, but if you're an empath, you must learn to protect yourself from absorbing too much negative energy. You'll want to help everyone because you can feel the things they can't even articulate but always remember: you can't pour from an empty cup.

● Energy Healing

Everything in the world has an energy or life force that flows through it, including the human body, and anytime this energy is blocked or disrupted, what you get is physical, emotional, or mental problems. If you're a healer with this gift, you can detect these blockages or imbalances. You have a sixth sense of where the energy isn't flowing correctly. You may feel a tingle; some healers see colors, and some can intuitively tell where the problem is. A natural healer can see that there is a problem, but only a trained healer can fix it. Luckily, natural healers gravitate towards healing professions, alternative or not, because of their desire to see people whole again. Some end up as doctors or nurses, some become reiki healers, others use crystals, and some even turn to herbalism. Whatever the route, their gift gives them the power to fix energetic imbalances by clearing the blockages and restoring the body's natural energy flow so that its healing mechanisms are kickstarted, which it then uses to repair itself.

● Clairvoyance

Clairvoyance, also called clear sight, is the supernatural ability to perceive information or events that are not available to the physical senses. It's a kind of extrasensory perception (ESP) that lets people retrieve information about the past or see and understand things that are not physically present. Clairvoyants see images, visions, or scenes far into the past and also in the present. If you're clairvoyant, you may have seen auras around people, conjured energy fields, or received intuitive downloads. Clairvoyance is intuition plus psychic abilities and a heightened level of awareness. Some people are just naturally more sensitive to the energies and information floating around in the collective consciousness. They can not only sense this information, they can plug into its source and channel it.

- **Clairaudience**

Clairaudience is the power to hear messages that others can't. Clairaudients have described this power as someone whispering secrets to you that only you can hear, and these whispers could come from spiritual guides, angels, or other non-physical entities. They hear actual voices that are gentle sometimes and urgent other times. You may not even hear voices; you just have a song pop into your mind, and you know intuitively that there is a message in the lyrics. This isn't imagination or wishful thinking. Clairaudients insist that what they hear is real and important. They're not mentally unstable; they're not hearing things; their ears are simply tuned into a higher frequency that connects them to universal consciousness.

- **Telepathy**

Dr. Charles Xavier is the perfect example of a telepath. Telepaths know what a person is thinking or feeling without being told. They can see into another person's mind, quite literally or intuitively. Like empaths, they read the thoughts, emotions, and exact physical sensations of the people in their immediate environment, and depending on how strong their telepathy is, they can reach minds that are miles away. A telepath knows exactly what you're about to say before you say it. They can also send their thoughts and ideas straight into someone else's mind without saying a word. It sounds too Hollywood, too unrealistic, but have you ever finished someone's sentence? Or felt that someone was thinking about you? Have you ever picked up the phone to call someone, only to find out they were just about to call you? You may not be a telepath, but everyone experiences telepathy to a degree. Telepaths aren't always right. Even with practice, it involves interpretation, and some messages get lost in translation. You've misinterpreted a text message at one point, right? Telepaths can also misinterpret thoughts or feelings, but they are supernaturally gifted nonetheless.

- **Precognition**

Skeptics have called precognition a coincidence or a trick of the mind, but is it so hard to believe that some people get glimpses of the future? There have been too many accurate seers in human history to dismiss this gift as ridiculous. We've had Nostradamus, Edgar Cayce, and Mother Shipton, and they have made predictions, including significant historical events, with no less than 80% accuracy. In the olden days, shamans and oracles were consulted for guidance on important decisions, like when to plant or when to go to war. Their predictions were not treated lightly because they somehow could reach into a space beyond time for knowledge that other people couldn't get to. People still visit psychics today to get readings about love, their future or the past.

You don't have to be proclaimed an oracle or a prophet to know you are psychic. A psychic could wake up one morning with a strong need to call their friend, then find out later that day their friend was in an accident. You could have a vivid dream about a natural disaster and then see it happen on the news a few weeks later. This kind of power can be comforting but also worrying because some psychics, and probably because they are psychics, would rather not know the future.

- **Manifestation**

Manifestation is the process of bringing your thoughts, wishes, and desires into 3D reality. It's the ability to harness the power of your mind to create the life you want to live. Everybody can manifest to a degree because thoughts and emotions hold power, and everyone feels and thinks. The difference between those who manifest quickly and those who don't is in the focus, consistency, and beliefs they have. Effective manifestation begins with your mindset. You need to believe that you have the power to create your dream life. This is harder than it looks because the Matrix conditions you to believe that your circumstances are out of your control, and it doesn't help if your waking reality seems so far removed from that dream life. But everything seen and unseen is energy, and energy can be manipulated – never created or destroyed, but manipulated. If you can manipulate your thoughts and feelings, you can shift the energy around you. Manifestation is a supernatural gift that draws from the abundant, creative energy of the universe, giving you the permission to consciously co-create your reality. Unlike intuition, this is the hardest supernatural gift to unlock.

Where Do Supernatural Gifts Come From?

Your divine spark is the source of your supernatural gifts. We've covered the spark in chapter 3 if you need a refresher. The divine spark is your eternal, spiritual core that is forever linked to the Pleroma. It is not bound by the 3D or the construct of the ego, so by default, it has access to realms and abilities that far surpass the normal human experience.

Besides being the reason for your divinity, your divine spark is also a conduit that channels the infinite potential of the Pleroma into this tangible 3D world. If your connection to your spark is stronger and you are more aligned with it, the more energy it can channel and the more extraordinary the abilities you can harness.

Divine realms and things of the spirit are, by their very nature, past the scope of humanity's current scientific understanding, but where science fails, ancient wisdom comes through. Spiritual traditions and esoteric teachings of old understood the divine spark to be a gateway to higher states of consciousness – dimensions that are not apparent to the five senses. Thanks to your divine spark, you have the key to a door that opens into these dimensions. Your consciousness expands, and you can suddenly reach into these spaces and manipulate energy in ways that defy the Matrix.

These dimensions have always existed, only previously invisible to you and others unawakened. When you activate them, your supernatural gifts don't come from nothing. They are a natural extension of your divine spark. Everyone has the potential for these gifts, but not everyone is aware of them. Benson Boone could've sworn he couldn't sing, but then he never tried until one day he did, and a little over a year later, his first song was charting in 16 countries. Five years later, he's a Grammy nominee. You don't think you have supernatural gifts, but it could be that you've never actually bothered with dimensions other than this one.

This is not an encouragement to do anything crazy. Do NOT attempt to jump off a building; you will not fly. The supernatural gifts we talk about here are more energetic than anything. The laws of physics are very real, and they still apply even to the supernaturally gifted. Your gifts allow energetic manipulation that circumvents the belief in what's possible, but when all is said and done, you're still bound by the same 3D laws that govern everyone else. Use your gifts with humility, wisdom, and respect for the natural order because with great power comes great responsibility.

Obstacles to Your Divine Activation

- **Fear and Doubt:** You can't activate your gifts if you're afraid of them or if you don't believe you have them in the first place. Fear and doubt shut the door before you even get a chance to touch the handle. Fear stops you from trying, and doubt tells you that if you try, you'll fail. It'll sound convincingly true when your mind tells you that these gifts are a fantasy, and even if they're not, you're not worthy or capable of accessing them. To beat this, you need faith – faith in yourself and faith in what you believe. Faith requires self-acceptance. Accept yourself, gifts or not. It is through this acceptance that you find your gifts because you do have them; everyone does. It's normal to be afraid, but your fear doesn't define your potential.

- **The Ego's Attachment to Illusions:** The ego craves control, validation, and the comfort that comes with familiarity. It doesn't like surrendering its grip on what it defines as its identity. It's the ego that clings to the material world, to the self as a separate, somewhat selfish entity, and to the Matrix and its expectations that keep you confined. You threaten the ego every time you connect with your divine spark. You threaten it with a loss of control, with the dismantling of the carefully constructed reality it has worked so hard to maintain. Activating your supernatural gifts is a threat, and so it will fight back like a stubborn child. Self-awareness is the only way out of this illusion. You must know yourself through shadow work. Shadow work observes and integrates the subconscious self that the ego tries to suppress or deny. Everyone who has observed their ego eventually discovered one thing: they held on just as tightly to their ego as the ego does to them, and they realized that all they needed to do was let go. Your ego is a cluster of illusions that feeds on more illusions. Sort through the mess and find freedom in the space that is left.

- **Energetic Blockages:** Energy can not be manipulated if it isn't allowed to flow. Energetic blockages cause resistance and resistance limits access to your supernatural gifts. Blockages manifest as muscle tension, emotional stagnation, or disconnection from universal energy. You need to restore your energy flow if you hope to activate your gifts. Energy work like chakra balancing, crystal cleansing, breathwork, emotional release, and so on works wonders for this sort of problem. If you can unblock and align the energy centers in your body, you can make a clear, unobstructed channel for the divine spark to express itself through your supernatural gifts. You may need to confront and release generational traumas, heal emotional wounds, or just love yourself, none of which are easy. But they are necessary for your peace and spiritual evolution.

How to Activate Your Supernatural Gifts

- **Cultivating Awareness**

Activating your supernatural gifts when you don't know what they are is next to impossible, and to know what they are, you must first know what/who you are. Self-awareness is developed through paying attention to your thoughts, feelings, and physical sensations. Mindfulness through meditation will clear your head and help you concentrate on the energies inside you. It won't happen right away, but as you get better at it, you'll see signs of your gifts, and then you'll know where to direct your activation energy.

- **Purifying Your Energy**

Supernatural gifts are strongest when your energy is clear and positive, meaning you need to cleanse your energy field to activate your gifts. This cleansing could be energy healing or rituals to balance your chakras and remove negative energies. Your energy is best kept at a high vibration for your supernatural gifts to manifest.

- **Strengthening Your Connection to the Divine**

Supernatural gifts connect you to a higher power or universal consciousness. Activating your connection to this source requires a genuine relationship with the divine. This happens through prayer, meditation, or shamanic rituals that place you in alignment with positive energy. You need to trust the divine because that is the equivalent of trusting your gifts.

Prayer allows you to connect to the divine.[48]

- **Practicing Regularly**

Activating and developing your supernatural gifts will not happen in a week. There's a reason they say Rome wasn't built in a day. Things of substance take time and consistent effort. You have to practice as many times as you can to strengthen your intuition and refine your abilities. This process is gradual, so you will need all the patience you can muster, but it will be worth it when your gifts flow through you with more authority than you ever thought was possible.

- **Using the Gifts for Service:**

Your supernatural gifts are there to help others and contribute to the greater good. The divine gave you this gift because you have a role to play in dismantling the Matrix and guiding souls to freedom. It may not seem like it, but every positive energy you send out into the world ripples through the collective consciousness. When you use your gifts to heal yourself or heal someone else, you heal a portion of the collective. The gift is yours, and you ultimately decide how you want to use it, but instead of feeding the Matrix, why not use it to serve something bigger than yourself? Why not use it to heal the world one soul at a time? It is always your choice.

Intuition Activation Exercises

- **Zener Cards:** Zener cards, also called ESP (Extra-Sensory Perception) cards, are a fun way to test and develop your intuitive gifts. Zener cards have simple shapes like circles, stars, or wavy lines printed on them. All you have to do is shuffle the deck, do a spread, and look at each card one by one. Try to guess what shape is on a card, then turn it over. This helps you train your psychic powers to perceive information without your conventional senses.

Zener Cards.[48]

- **Tarot Card Reading:** Tarot cards are a deck of illustrated cards with meanings assigned to each card, but how they are interpreted has more to do with symbolism and intuition on the reader's part. Performing an intuitive reading with a tarot deck is one way to train your intuition. It helps to know the standard meaning of each card as background knowledge, but the whole point is allowing your intuition to determine the interpretation. Ask your question and shuffle the deck. Intuitively select a few or shuffle until one flies out, then use your intuition to read the cards for answers.

Tarot Cards."

- **Psychometry (Energy Sensing):** Psychometry is the power to read the energy or history of an object by physically touching it. For this exercise, ask a friend to borrow you a personal item, maybe jewelry or a pen. Rub your palms together for 30 seconds to activate your own energy, and then hold the object in your bare hands. Wait and see if you feel any sensations or emotions from it. You could even get visions about the owner or something related to the object. When you're done, tell your friend what you saw or felt to see how accurate you were.

Dreamwork for Precognition

Precognition is the power to see the future before it happens, and the dreamscape is where most precognitive messages come in through. Here's how you can train this gift using dreamwork:

Step 1: Remember Your Dreams

First off, what kind of seer are you if you can't remember your dreams, you know? When you wake up, the first thing you should do is take a few minutes to recall as much detail as you can. Write them down in a dream journal.

Step 2: Identify the Emotions

While writing down your dreams, pinpoint the emotions you felt. Make a list of all the different feelings you had in the dream and the order in which they happened. This shows the emotional flow of the dream. For example, you might have felt sad, then curious, then confused, then afraid, and then relieved. The sequence in which the emotions come in can tell you a lot about what the dream is trying to reveal to you.

Step 3: Compare Your Dreams

Don't focus on one dream; that's a rookie mistake. Look at a series of your recent dreams. What patterns do you see? Are there any repeating symbols, characters, or circumstances? How are your emotions and reactions changing from dream to dream? Follow the progression and development across multiple dreams. What are the connecting themes? Write them down.

Step 4: Shift Your Perspective

Consider looking at your dreams from another angle, not just the dreamer's perspective. Replay the dream but through the eyes of another character or element in the dream. If you dreamt you were being chased by a bear, and then you tripped over a log, turned around, and saw the bear change into a woman, replay the dream again, but this time as the bear or even as the log. How would they see things? How will they tell the story? This can help you from seeing the dream as happening TO you. A dream is an interaction between all the parts, including you. Shifting your viewpoint can show you an interpretation you might be missing.

Step 5: Write It Down and Wait

Write down the dream and your interpretations in your dream journal. If you don't have any interpretations, don't force it. If it comes, it comes.

However, pay attention over the next few weeks to see if any elements from the dream show up in your waking reality. It doesn't have to be literal; it could be an intuitive reminder of the dream. When that happens, go back to your journal because there's a connection somewhere.

Chapter 7: Navigating Higher Dimensions of Reality

Can you imagine for a second that you are a flat circle living on a flat piece of paper? This is the only world you've ever known – a 2D plane with length and width but no height or depth. You can only move left and right because your awareness is limited. You can't possibly conceive what it means to go up into a third dimension because there is no height. From your perspective, the world is flat, and that is all there is. Now, let's say someone picks up the paper and folds it into a 3D shape, a cube, for instance, and just like that, there is a new dimension – height. Being the flat circle, you would have no way to perceive or comprehend this new dimension. It would be completely foreign and outside the scope of your limited 2D existence, but that doesn't make it any less real, does it?

It's time to navigate the higher dimension of your reality.[45]

This is how humans define higher dimensions. They are worlds that exist outside the three dimensions (length, width, height) that we directly recognize as reality. Just as the flat circle could not imagine a third dimension, it is almost impossible for you to completely imagine or understand dimensions that are above or below this current 3D world. 3D objects like cubes, spheres, or pyramids are easy to identify and explain, but how do you explain a fourth dimension?

Some consider time to be in the fourth dimension. You can see how objects change over time, but you cannot see time itself. The flat circle cannot perceive height for the same reasons you can't grasp how time interacts with the three spatial dimensions you know.

Mathematicians and physicists have tried their best to study higher dimensions. A fourth dimension has been successfully represented mathematically, but picturing it is still dicey. A 4D hypercube, also called a tesseract, is a shape that extends the 3D cube into four dimensions. You can't see it in the same way you can see a cube, but you can study and sort of understand its properties through equations and models.

If you project a 3D object into 2D space, maybe a cube (again), it'll look like a square in 2D. A tesseract can be illustrated in 3D as a cube within a cube, connected at the corners. This illustration helps show the complexity of higher dimensions, even if you can't exactly see them. You can apply this to emotions as well. You can feel happiness, sadness, anger, and peace, but these feelings are not tangible. You can't hold them in your hand.

Higher Dimensions and Consciousness

Everything in the universe is energy, and everything vibrates. Then, depending on how fast the vibration is, that energy is made manifest in a particular form. Every dimension corresponds to a separate frequency (speed of vibration). It happens with sound waves, but it has also been observed in light, colors, and even emotions, so why not consciousness?

Consciousness is the one thing responsible for awareness. It is what makes experience possible. You can see, touch, and feel because you possess a consciousness that renders you conscious. However, what you CAN see, touch, and feel is also limited BY your consciousness.

Consciousness is a spectrum, and at one end, you have basic awareness. This level of consciousness allows you to take in stimuli from your environment and produce a reaction. Going further along this spectrum, you'll find deeper awareness. If your consciousness is around this level on the spectrum, it means you understand not just who you are but also who you are in relation to other people and the universe as a whole. Think of it as you've moved from seeing the Met Gala outfits on the red carpet to watching the Vogue BTS - the Get Ready With Me(s) - and discovering the details and the story behind every look.

Higher levels of consciousness are found in higher dimensions because they vibrate at a higher frequency. Dimensions that operate at this level are invisible and mostly incomprehensible to 3D lifeforms. There are beings who live there, much like there are beings here, and they go about their activities much like we do here, except for one thing. You can't see them or their dimension. So, as far as your five senses know, they are not real, but they are, and they exist right alongside this reality, a three-dimensional one. Here, you can move forward, backward, left, right, up, and down, but in higher dimensions, the entities or beings that live there operate on frequencies your brain can't even comprehend. They aren't bound by the rules of time and space as you know them. For us, time flows in a straight line - there is the past, the present, and the future - but for these higher beings, time might be more like a soup where everything happens at the same time. You may not be able to see them, but from the little that is understood about higher dimensions, they can see you just fine. They can also influence this reality through mechanisms you may not consciously be aware of.

The Purpose of Higher Dimensions During Spiritual Awakening

Higher dimensions are your way out of the Matrix: The highest dimension is the Pleroma, and it is a space of pure divine light and consciousness. This dimension stands in contrast to the 3D world, a dense dimension that is known for illusion and separation from the divine. The purpose of a spiritual awakening is to ascend to higher dimensions, and this ascension begins with your consciousness. When your consciousness vibrates at a higher frequency, even if you are physically bound to the 3D world until your vessel expires, the veil of Maya dissolves. Maya is the reason you see the world as separate, solid objects. It is the reason you believe that you are disconnected from each other and from a higher power. After the curtain is pulled back, things that once seemed random or meaningless reveal themselves to be interconnected. Higher dimensions invite you to rise above Maya to a frequency where there is no separation, only source – only peace.

Higher dimensions are sources of wisdom and creativity: Moving higher up through dimensions, you not only see reality more clearly, but you also find wisdom and creativity, unlike anything in the 3D. The Akashic records are in a library believed to contain every knowledge of everything from the beginning of time, and some say into the future as well. This library is not a place you can go to like your town library. It is on an entirely different dimension, and you need to step into a higher level of consciousness to get there. In places like these, or higher dimensions in general, the line between your thoughts and the universal mind is thinnest – so thin that collective wisdom flows freely back and forth between the two. To better understand this, let's say you have a problem, and you settle down to meditate on your problem (and sometimes you don't even have to). Your consciousness, vibrating at a high frequency, blends with the universal mind. Now, because there is nothing truly unknown in the universe, the solution (already floating in the universal consciousness) penetrates your skull into your mind and then into your awareness. This is what they call divine inspiration.

Higher dimensions strengthen your connection to divine and universal consciousness: If everything in existence could fit into a tall building, this reality (the 3D) would be the ground floor. The universe is multidimensional, and you are a multidimensional entity trapped in a three-dimensional vessel. This 3D vessel, your body, is the only reason you can interact with the third dimension. It definitely has its limitations, but without it, there would be no "experience," so to speak. The soul is not confined to the 3D like the body is. It is free to take the elevator to the next floor and the floor after that and so on, but the soul, being in a 3D vessel, believes IT is as limited as the meat suit it currently wears. That is fair, to be honest, because if you're on a bike cruising down the freeway, you're not wrong to think you have to go only where the road allows, but nobody said you can't park your bike on the side of the road and walk into the woods. Ascending to higher dimensions doesn't change your physical location. It can't as long as you have a 3D body. Your consciousness is what goes up and down the building, and from a higher vantage point in the building, you can see a lot more than when you were on the ground floor. You can see more people and how streets connect to one another. You can see the bus zooming down the road from three blocks away – you can see more, and that is not even the divine's view because you're not remotely high enough. Still, you're much closer to the divine than you were before, and your connection is much stronger.

Signs You Are Experiencing a Higher Dimension

• Increased Synchronicities and Intuitive Insights

The single most noticeable sign that your awareness/consciousness has expanded to a higher dimension will be the explosion of synchronicities. For example, you could be seeing the color blue like it's following you – blue cars, blue butterflies, blue logos, blue coffee mugs – and later that week, you get an impromptu invitation to a party, and you're given two outfits to choose from. A blue one and a green one. You're likely to choose the blue one because in that moment, it makes sense why you've been haunted by that color for the past week. Intuition is also heightened when you're connected to higher dimensions. Your gut feelings become stronger and more accurate – so accurate that your decisions are now made based on a feeling over logic, like deciding to take a new route home because something tells you it's safer, and later, you hear about an accident on your usual route. Connecting with higher dimensions means you found the elevator out of the ground floor, and that puts you at least two steps ahead because now you have a better vantage point.

• Vivid Dreams

If your frequency is high enough, your dreams will feel more real than your waking life. And that is because the dreamscape (the astral plane) is equally as real as the 3D, yet you're conditioned to treat it as irrelevant, as just a dream. Every time you dream, your consciousness goes to a space where the Matrix's rules don't apply. You can fly, meet people who have passed away or go to places you've never been to. In the dream world, one thing means another, and you have memories you don't remember making in places you don't recognize. There is much we don't know about higher dimensions, but we do know that a stronger connection to these dimensions almost always equals colorful, detailed, and emotionally charged dreams. You receive messages in the astral plane – messages that can only be interpreted intuitively, messages that do not make sense in the Matrix. They say dreams are a window to the subconscious, and they're not wrong, but dreams are also a language on their own. They're a portal to another dimension – one that was always unmistakable; it was you who wasn't as connected.

Vivid dreams can contain emotionally charged messages.⁴⁶

• Timelessness

Time feels linear in 3D – you wake up, go about your day, you go to sleep, and you wake up to do it all over again. Life down here is measured by ticking clocks, calendars, and schedules, so you'll know you're aligned with a higher dimension when linear time disappears and the clock has stopped ticking. Dreams, which have been established to be a higher dimension, are one of the places where time stretches, compresses, and, depending on the circumstance, loops. Either way, one moment doesn't lead to the next, not the way it does in 3D. You can dream an entire lifetime when you've only been asleep for five minutes. Why? Because time is more flexible than you think, especially outside the 3D. There's no urgency, no pressure. Everything has happened, is happening, and will happen all at the same time. Higher dimensional awareness releases your attachment to the linear progression of time to show you just how malleable time is and how connected everything is to everything else.

Common Barriers to Accessing Higher Dimensions

Knowing and accepting that higher dimensions exist parallel to this reality is only half the work it takes to actually get to these dimensions. Here are a few things that could delay your ascension:

- **Fear of the unknown:** There is safety in the familiar. You know what to expect and what is expected of you. Any dimension other than the 3D is the opposite of familiar, and for good reason. 3D rules are precise; you know what is possible and what isn't, and your brain is conditioned to reject otherwise. However, these same rules are considered primitive and limited in higher dimensions. Many people would rather stick to what they know and trust than knowingly risk doing something as "dangerous" as accessing another dimension.

- **Attachments to the physical realm:** This world is defined by material possessions, and so the inhabitants of this world are also defined by their material possessions. Jesus himself said that it is difficult for the rich to enter the kingdom of heaven (Matthew 19:23-24). This has less to do with the riches themselves and more to do with the attachment to said riches. Attachment binds you to the 3D and keeps higher dimensions just out of reach.

- **Energetic blockages from unhealed emotions:** In ancient Egypt, they had something called the principle of maat, where upon your death, your heart would be weighed against a feather to determine if you would move on to paradise. You can take this literally or choose to see it as a metaphor for how you carry emotional burdens throughout your life. A heart that is carrying anger, guilt, bitterness, jealousy, and so on is considered too heavy to ascend to higher dimensions. Energetic blockages are created when you don't confront your feelings, and these blockages keep you from experiencing life to the fullest. In a way, these blockages are attachments. You're attached to your anger, to your pain, to vengeance, and these emotions clog your energy channels and keep you stuck in the 3D. They are chained to you as much as you are to them, and they will remain an anchor until you cut them loose.

Quick Tips for Overcoming These Barriers

- Don't force a new spiritual experience; ease into it. Give yourself time to adjust.

- Declutter every once in a while. Get rid of anything you don't need. It may seem easy enough until you have to give away something you don't need but are quite attached to.

- Make self-reflection an automatic response to every circumstance. This can help you process your emotions at the moment and identify unhealed wounds, if there are any.

- Forgive more.

- Curiosity is often a better response than frustration.

- Watch your media consumption. Try as much as possible to avoid fear-propagating content and lean more towards wholesomeness and love.

Dimensional Expansion Visualization

1. Find a comfortable chair and settle in.

2. Plant your bare feet firmly on the ground and take three deep breaths, then close your eyes.

3. Imagine you're a tree. Feel the ground underneath your feet. Is it cold or warm? Is it smooth, or is there grass under your feet?

4. Imagine your feet sinking into the ground until all your toes are submerged. You should feel a tingle in your toes as roots extend out of them and into the ground below. These roots connect you to the soil. Feel this connection. Feel the nutrients and minerals flowing from the ground into your roots and through your trunk. You are quite literally grounded in place, and there is nothing to be afraid of.

5. Next, let your branches reach upwards, growing and extending to the sky. Feel your leaves unfurling and spreading out to capture the sunlight. Physically stretch your arms so you feel the open space above you.

6. Feel your branches continue to grow, reaching further and further into space, where they split and divide to form a sprawling network that seems to reach everywhere and every dimension. With this

expansion, you can quite literally feel your connection with the universe on your skin. There are no more physical limits; your trunk – your soul – is expanding. Time and space seem to bend and warp around you. Past, present, and future converge in this moment, where you finally allow yourself to take up space. Fill the room, fill the universe.

7. Breathe deeply in and out, and feel the energy pulsing through you. It is the same energy that animates the very stars. You are not separate from the universe. Your consciousness radiates outwards from your physical form. You are simultaneously infinitesimal and infinite, a microcosm and a macrocosm. Remain like this for as long as you like.

8. When you're done, slowly retract your branches and guide them back to your trunk. The universe, as infinite as it is, is still there, but for now, your focus should return to your 3D vessel.

9. Take one last deep breath, and open your eyes.

Interconnectedness Meditation

1. Take a deep, steadying breath and close your eyes.

2. Pay attention to how your body feels right now – the slow rise and fall of your stomach as you breathe, the air moving in and out through your nose.

3. Settle into this quiet, meditative state and try to expand your awareness to the things outside your physical self.

4. Start with the space around you; think about it. Feel the air and energy in the room. You can't see it, but that space is very much there, and in a way, it connects you to everything else.

5. Open your eyes, but try not to zoom in on any one thing. Let your gaze take in the whole scene in front of you. Look at how the colors and shapes blend and overlap to form a cohesive image. There aren't any clear edges or boundaries; everything flows seamlessly into the next.

6. Are there any sounds you hear? Don't hone in on a single noise; just listen. If you're outside, you may hear leaves rustling or a car driving by. These sounds, different as they are, are one melody. You're part of that melody, not separate from it.

7. Picture yourself stepping outside of this world you're in. Remove yourself from the familiar things and situations that normally constitute your life. What is left? How do you feel? What do you notice in this new expanded space?

8. Expanded as you are, remember that you're still connected to everything. You're not a singular, isolated entity. You're a spoke in a much larger wheel. You belong here. There's a place for you. Your presence matters.

9. Whenever you want to end the session, come back into your body and open your eyes.

Astral Travel

Astral projection is the process of separating your astral body from your physical body, and astral travel happens when you astral project. Notice it says the separation of the astral body, not the soul. The astral body and the soul are not the same thing. The astral body is a duplicate or energetic copy of your physical body. Unlike your physical body, which is flesh, bones, and blood, the astral body is non-physical matter.

When you astral project, your consciousness detaches from your physical body and shifts into this astral body, which it then uses to astral travel. Your astral body looks exactly like your physical body, except it's transparent and bright at the same time, almost like it's glowing from the inside. Also, like the physical body, your astral body has its own anatomy. It has energetic centers (chakras) that regulate energy flow and an energetic circulatory system called nadis to carry this life-force energy throughout the body.

Since the astral body is more lightweight and flexible than the physical, it can travel distances in the blink of an eye. It can pass through solid objects and fly. Colors are brighter, sounds are clearer, and you're more aware in your astral body. However, it is still a vessel like your physical body.

The soul is eternal; it can never die. It is permanent and unchanging. The astral body, on the other hand, is a ghostly duplicate of the physical body, and it depends on it (the physical body) to exist. Everything in the 3D has an astral form – animals, trees, even water – and when the physical counterpart ceases to exist, the astral duplicate becomes an empty shell that decays and dies.

Your consciousness can ascend to higher dimensions, and sometimes, it uses your astral body to do that, and even then, the astral body doesn't completely detach from the physical body. Despite your awareness shifting from one vessel to the other, both vessels remain connected through a silver cord that keeps your astral form tethered to your physical form. The silver cord is an energetic lifeline that makes sure your physical body and all its vital functions are safe and intact, at the same time guaranteeing your astral body finds its way back home.

Nobody astral projects on the first try, partly because of the mental conditioning we've been talking about but also because it may very well be the scariest thing you've ever experienced – at least, at first. Your limbs will feel heavy, and your entire body will vibrate like an old phone, amongst other things. It will scare any beginner. Your mind and body are being asked to do something they've never done before, so some initial fear or resistance is to be expected. If you can make it past the initial sensations and successfully split, you will feel freer than you have ever felt, possibly in your whole life.

How to Astral Project

Astral projection is complicated, and people have come up with so many techniques to successfully switch vessels and detach, but there is one that has worked most of all. You need to induce sleep paralysis first, then detach. Start here:

1. Finding the right position is non-negotiable. You can lie on your back, but you may have better luck lying on your side.

2. Before you start, do a big stretch. Roll your shoulders, wiggle your toes, flex your knees – whatever feels good to release the tension in your body.

3. Now, settle in and try to stay as still as possible. Breathe slowly into your stomach and out.

4. Let your body relax.

5. Listen for a faint hum in the background that you normally wouldn't notice.

6. If you feel a slight urge to move – like you want to change positions – resist that impulse and stay still. Your body is trying to fall asleep, even while your mind remains awake and alert.

7. It might take a while, up to an hour and a half even, but stick with it.

8. You'll know you've done it when your body starts vibrating. Don't panic; just remain calm and observant. You are still fully conscious even though you can't move right now.

9. Imagine a rope dangling above you and try to reach for it. Remember, you can't move your physical arms or your legs, but you can still reach for the rope. Try to grab it.

10. When you do, hold on to it and try to climb the rope.

11. After what feels like a minute or two of climbing, look down. Your body should be lying still like you're sleeping while you are now floating above it. There'll be a silver cord linking you both, and the rope from earlier will have disappeared. You have successfully detached from your physical vessel and are now ready for astral travel.

Tips for Traveling Through Higher Dimensions

- Before you attempt any sort of interdimensional travel, know your purpose. Know why you're doing this. Are you trying to learn something, raise your frequency, or something else? Your purpose will keep you grounded.

- Conjure a sphere of light to surround your whole body. This sphere is an energetic shield to keep you safe from negativity.

- Don't spend too much time in the higher realms in the beginning. Your initial explorations should be short and intentional, like 10 to 15 minutes max.

- If you ever feel anxious, just breathe and remind yourself that you are safe and there is nothing to fear.

- However, if something feels terribly wrong, don't ignore it. Trust your gut and stop what you're doing. You're not giving in to fear; you're applying wisdom.

- Don't overthink or analyze every little thing that happens. Let the experience play out naturally.

- Always come back slowly. Take the time to gently reorient yourself back into 3D.

- Drink water before, during, and after your sessions. It also helps to have a light snack nearby, like grapes or biscuits.

Chapter 8: Recalling Reincarnations and Other Lives

The best way to understand the cycle of reincarnation is to think of it as a wheel. Your soul is the hub, and a single lifetime is a spoke. With every turn of the wheel, your soul stays in place while lifetimes come and go. A lifetime is a temporary manifestation of your soul's expression in the physical world. When that life is over, the wheel turns, and that spoke disappears into the past as a new one comes forth with a new life.

Reincarnation is at the center of many different belief systems.[47]

One of the world's oldest religions has reincarnation right at the center of its belief system, and that religion is Hinduism. Hindus believe that when you die, your atman(soul) doesn't die with the physical body; it is freed from it to be reborn in a new body. This is a cycle that continues through lifetimes until you achieve moksha or liberation from the wheel of samsara.

Right beside reincarnation, they believe in karma. They believe that your actions have consequences that follow you from one life to the next, and every lifetime is an opportunity to purify your karma through good thoughts, words, and actions. Once you are purified, your soul is no longer subject to the cycle of reincarnation, and you are reunited with Braham (Source).

Not all religions believe in reincarnation and karma the way Hindus do. Some believe in a little bit of this, while others preach a little bit of that. However, in most religions, there is a general belief in the continuity of the soul, in the fact that mortal life is not the entirety of human existence. There is a shared conviction that there is something more, some continued spiritual reality after this physical life. Basically, the majority of the human race refuses to accept that death is the end. Good for us then that it isn't.

Past Lives

Your soul does not belong to any one religion, ethnicity, or race. It is timeless and not exclusive to this brief lifetime. It has existed for far longer and taken on several forms and experiences across too many incarnations. Your soul has inhabited bodies all over the planet, in every corner of the world, throughout every era in history. It is a traveler, and you have more memories than you can even put into words. The people you know in this lifetime – your family, your friends, lovers? Chances are you've known most, if not all, of them before, in previous lives. You have relationships that stretch back through incarnations. Some karmic, some not quite, but either way, you're drawn to these people because, to some degree, you recognize them.

Some souls are very old and have been reincarnating for millions of years. Others have only a few lifetimes under their belt, and some are new baby souls. Earth isn't the only planet where a soul can incarnate to have a 3D experience. In fact, many souls who have been reincarnating for a while have never had a lifetime on Earth. It used to be relatively rare for brand-new souls to be incarnating on Earth - brand-new in the sense that they have never been here before - but it seems these days, they're coming in droves. We increasingly see beings from other star systems and dimensions choosing to take on physical form and live a human life. Their mission is to assist humanity and raise the collective consciousness.

Who knows, you might be one of them, or maybe you're an old Earth soul who has done this many times. Old souls are ancient and wise beyond their years, even as children. They've been around the block, so they know things and are not at all sure where the knowledge is from. You can be an old soul AND a starseed with a thousand incarnations in faraway star systems and knowledge that would make a typical Earthling seem crude and naive. Your soul might remember lifetimes on planets where the water was a different color and there were two suns in the sky, but you're on Earth now, here on a mission.

Starseeds are souls that have spent lifetimes outside the Matrix among higher vibrational races in dimensions where time is not real. They are here at this time to trigger an awakening, a collective shift that will free as many souls as possible and help the planet ascend from the 3D to 4D and 5D. This is their soul mission, and for the most part, this mission is tied to a previous incarnation or incarnations - it is tied to a past life.

Past Life Regression

Past life regression is a therapeutic process that uses hypnosis to send you into an altered state of consciousness for the sole purpose of accessing past life memories that are buried deep in your subconscious. The subconscious mind is a repository that holds the records of all your lived experiences, including those from previous lifetimes. Its capacity for processing information is nothing short of extraordinary, and honestly, you'd be lost without it.

At any given second, there is a deluge of information rushing into your brain all at once. This is everything from sounds, images, smells, sensations, impressions, and so on. The conscious mind can only handle a limited amount of data at a time because, frankly, it has more important things to do, like get you through the day. The subconscious mind, however, is a very busy bee sorting through all of that sensory input and deciding what's important and what can be safely ignored. Sometimes, it takes over previously conscious behaviors, makes them unconscious, and then activates them at the appropriate cues. Your habits or routines seem like conscious decision-making, but they're not. Your conscious mind is too busy keeping you upright and functional to be in charge of brushing your teeth or taking off your shoes.

This division of labor between the conscious and subconscious minds is sheer perfection. If you're in a crowded cafe with your mom, your conscious mind will focus exclusively on your mom's voice, while your subconscious automatically ignores the background chatter and street noise. You think you don't hear them, but you do. Your ears pick up on every single sound, including your mom's voice, the slurping and conversations from the table behind yours, including the laughter right outside your window. You would be overwhelmed if you consciously had to process all of that while listening to your mom, but you don't, thankfully. The subconscious takes that information and tucks it away for later. It has done this for you lifetime after lifetime. It is a hard drive with unlimited capacity, and it never sleeps.

A past life regression therapist guides you through this unlimited memory bank to retrieve information that you are not consciously aware that you have. This information is meant to fill in the blanks for you because the past is key to understanding the present. Your past lives are inextricably linked to your current life. You could say they flow into one another – tributaries that feed into a massive lake. Past life regression is how you draw from each tributary to understand your soul, the single constant through what could be a million lifetimes.

Benefits of Recalling Past Lives

- **Discovering emotional wounds from the past:** Past life regression can give you context for the emotional issues you're currently going through. If you almost drowned when you were 7, that memory is stored somewhere in your subconscious. You were only a child, and you didn't know you could drown, so you jumped into the deep end of the pool. You're older now, and you know there is a shallow end, but you still won't get in a pool because your subconscious remembers, in HD, the one time you almost drowned. This is one memory from one lifetime. Imagine 25 significant memories – each from at least 200 lifetimes – all stored in your subconscious. Your fears and trauma could very well come from previous lifetimes. Finding the source of your pain is the first step to healing and letting go.

- **Solving mysteries about yourself:** Like your fears, you have habits that appear to have come out of nowhere, but habits don't work like that. Past life regression can reveal the reason for your mysterious habits because there IS a reason. Some people don't care, but for those who want clarity, you're likely to find them in your subconscious.

- **Finally, understanding the reason for your relationships:** Memories from a person's childhood are enough to determine the outcomes of their adult relationships, so it's not exactly far-fetched to conclude that memories from a former lifetime could do the same thing. That aside, you have soul agreements in this incarnation that bind you to other souls, especially the ones closest to you. If you remember anything from Chapter 5, you'll know that a chunk of your soul agreements revolve around karmic lessons and soul evolution. There are people you meet in this life because of connections you've had in previous ones. You know in your soul you were meant to cross paths; what you don't know is why. Recalling your past lives can show you why.

- **Gaining a broader perspective on life:** This life is not all that there is or all that has been. You came into this world without a clue why you're here, what you're meant to be doing, or where you came from. Recalling your past lives could put this life into perspective for you. The realization that life is about more than this one lifetime could take the pressure off a little. You stop taking things personally and finally see the bigger picture. There's more to your story, and you have all of eternity to figure it out.

Signs of Past Life Memories

- **Realistic dreams or visions:** If, when you go to sleep, you have dreams that feel too real, as if you're reliving something that actually happened to you before, it could be a memory from a past life.

- **Unexplained emotional reactions:** Are there specific places, objects, or periods in history that provoke strong emotional reactions out of you with no logical reason whatsoever? You may very well have a connection to those things from a past life.

- **Déjà vu:** You know that feeling where it's like you've been somewhere or met someone before, but you literally just met for the first time? Déjà vu is almost always a sign of past-life memories.

- **Strange obsessions:** If you are repeatedly drawn to the same types of stories, historical eras, or spiritual beliefs despite them not being relevant to your current life, a subconscious memory from a past life could be the reason.

Barriers to Past Life Regression

- **Aphantasia:** Some people have a condition called aphantasia, which means they can't form visual memories. They can't use their mind's eye. The point of PLR is to imagine or see scenarios from your past lives, but for someone with aphantasia, there's a huge problem, considering they can't conjure mental images at all. This doesn't particularly stop them from seeing a PLR therapist; it just means they need an approach that doesn't involve visual recall. If you have aphantasia, you need to tell your therapist so they lean more towards emotional memories and physical sensations, not visions or images.

- **Doubt:** When it comes to past lives, there are many skeptics. They think it's made up or a fad. You could be one of these skeptics. Skepticism isn't a bad thing, but it is definitely a barrier to PLR therapy. To get past this, try to keep an open mind. Read stories from people who believe they've experienced past lives. See if you have any stories of your own that make you wonder if you've lived before. You don't have to believe it immediately; simply be open to the possibility without judging it.

- **Fears about what might be discovered:** Past life regression therapy is known for bringing up surprisingly potent emotions and shocking revelations. It's normal to feel scared about what you might find in your subconscious. This is why people work with professionals who guide them safely through the process. Your therapist will prepare you mentally and emotionally, but on your end, you need to take it slow and not rush into anything you're not ready for.

- **Restlessness and trouble focusing:** Past-life regression is a form of hypnotherapy, so you HAVE to relax. This is harder than you think for some people. They can't seem to relax for one reason or the other. Their minds are hyperactive and refuse to give in to hypnosis. If this sounds like you, practicing meditation will do you a lot of good, and not just for PLR therapy. Relaxation is good for the mind and body. It's an opportunity to reset and ground yourself. Let go and give your mind the peace it doesn't know it needs.

- **Unqualified professionals:** There are too many people out there who claim to be experts in past-life regression therapy but don't have any training or the proper credentials, and there are too many downsides to working with an unqualified therapist, the most annoying being wasting your time. Do your research before you settle for a therapist. Your best bet is someone with formal training in hypnotherapy and psychotherapy, plus some experience in PLR therapy. Everyone is an expert until you ask about their qualifications.

Self-Hypnosis Meditation: Past Life Regression

Record this script in your own voice to use as a guided meditation for self-hypnosis, and press play whenever you want to retrieve a past life memory.

1. Sit or lie down somewhere peaceful.
2. Breathe in and out, and feel the tension leaving your muscles.
3. Close your eyes and picture a staircase in your mind. It leads down into a gloomy hallway.
4. One step at a time, make your way down the stairs. Don't rush so you don't break your meditative focus.
5. At the bottom of the stairs, there's a long corridor with doors lining the walls on both sides. Each door will take you to a different past life.
6. Look at the doors for as long as you want. Try to get a feel of the energy and history behind each one.
7. You'll have to choose a door eventually, so choose one that calls to you or feels intuitively right.
8. Approach your door and place your hand on the handle. Turn the knob and pull the door open.
9. You should feel a shift in your whole body as you step through the doorway.

10. Look around. What kind of place is this? What era does it seem to be from? What are you wearing?

11. Can you find a mirror or bowl of water to see your reflection? What do you look like? Describe yourself out loud. How does it feel to inhabit this body from the past?

12. Who else is here with you? Do they feel familiar? How do you feel here? Are there any clues to what your role or purpose is?

13. Spend as much time as you like observing this past life, and take in as many details as you can.

14. The minute you would like to go back to your current timeline, imagine the doorway behind you and walk through it like you did before.

15. Retrace your steps down the hall and up the staircase.

16. Take deep breaths as you return to your current time and body.

17. Open your eyes.

Chapter 9: Exiting Plato's Cave: Your Journey to Freedom

This is the final chapter, and it is safe to say you have come so far. A while ago, you were quite like Plato's prisoners, chained to the cave and mistaking shadows on the wall for reality. It was your whole life; it was all you knew, so it's not your fault, but somehow something made you turn around. Maybe it was this book, maybe it was something before. Whatever it was, it set you on a path that changed your life forever. You can't go back to the cave now. You can't go back to pretending like you haven't seen the light. You know it's not the same as it was. The things you once believed to be true are now hollow and incomplete.

Leaving Plato's cave symbolizes your freedom.[48]

Leaving the cave means you had to confront your darkest fears, there's no other way. With every step you took toward the light, there must've been confusion and temptations to pull you back in because, as far as the Matrix is concerned, you don't belong out there. You belong in here, ignorant and under its thumb.

But you did the visualizations, the meditations, and you connected with your divine spark. Now, the cave is behind you, and for the first time, you understand all you have been missing. You realize how in the dark you were – how in the dark so many people still are. Parts of you had to die to get here, and while that was a loss, it was also a rebirth. The journey is far from over, but you're halfway home.

So far:

- How do you feel about your progress?
- What is the most difficult obstacle you've had to overcome yet?
- What lessons did you learn from that obstacle?
- Have you discovered anything new about yourself?
- What three emotions do you cycle through every day now?
- How do you handle frustration and doubt?
- Who or what inspires you to keep going?
- What new habits have you added to your inventory?
- How do you define success for yourself on this journey?
- Would you say you are free?

True Freedom

When someone asks you, "Would you say you're free?" what they're really wondering is, "Are you still afraid?" Fear is a natural human emotion, like joy, jealousy, and anger. It is a protective emotion, one that binds you as tightly as it wants to save you. It is sneaky, this one. It has you convinced that being afraid is the smart thing to do, but no emotion stands in the way of your freedom like fear, and because it is disguised as safety, you let it.

Freedom is not fearlessness or the privilege to do what you want. It is an ascension that happens from the inside out. You're on a path to liberation from the Matrix, but freedom will remain unattainable until you let go of the things that bind you – your need for approval, your fear of the unknown, your fear of yourself. Internal restraints are tighter than any external chains could ever be. To be truly free, you must detach from the Matrix and its illusions because there is something much better on the other side of your fear: authenticity.

Authenticity is freedom; it is love. It is a genuine expression of self that can only be achieved through divine alignment. You don't have to be fearless; that is unrealistic. You only need to stop letting those fears dictate your choices and behavior. You are bigger than your emotions, bigger than your fear, and much bigger than the Matrix. Your freedom is in the realization that you are just as divine as the Demiurge himself and twice as powerful because your light is not corrupted, and your connection to Source was never severed.

This freedom is not a destination. It is a process that unfolds in phases. Each phase comes bearing gifts dressed up as lessons, but that is life because every experience is meant to teach you something new about yourself. The lessons have been there since the very beginning, but people tend to be more attached to the outcome than the journey itself. The journey is the point. If you're too attached to where you think you should be, you miss out on the present, and the present is where true freedom is.

Principles of True Freedom

- **Take full responsibility for your thoughts, emotions, and actions:** True freedom begins with taking ownership of your life. You are accountable for your thought patterns, your emotional responses, and the choices you make. For the most part, your life is in your hands, so make conscious, intentional decisions that are in alignment with the life you want to live.

- **Integrate spiritual wisdom into your daily life:** Spirituality is not an escape plan, nor is it an excuse to withdraw from the world. Spirituality is meant to infuse your life with meaning and purpose. It is meant to connect you to your environment, not isolate you.

- **Trust your inner compass and inner voice to guide you through decisions and challenges:** Listen to and trust your intuition. This doesn't mean ignoring logic entirely. There is a balance between intuition and reason; you need to find it.

- **Remain open to new perspectives, practices, and knowledge:** Freedom depends on your openness and curiosity. The second you stop learning, that is when you walk yourself into a cage. There is always room for expansion, even if it doesn't seem like it.

- **Understand that freedom is not an isolated experience:** Your personal freedom is intrinsically linked to the freedom of everyone else, and your lifestyle should be a reflection of that. Emma Lazarus once said, "Until all of us are free, none of us are free." So, what can you do to free your community?

Guided Meditation to Release Attachment

1. Get into a relaxing position, whatever that means for you. You can sit on the floor, in a chair, or anywhere your body can relax.

2. As always, you'll begin with a few deep breaths. Use the inhale to expand your belly and the exhale to release.

3. Focus on your body now. Concentrate on how it feels at this very moment. If there are any sensations or emotions, simply observe them. Don't judge. They are transient experiences, not a reflection of you. Let them come and go.

4. When your mind is free and calm, think about an area in your life where you're clinging to an outcome or attachment. You could have a goal you're working towards, a relationship you're hoping will last, or an expectation for how your life should be. Hold this thought without judgment and breathe in and out.

5. Can you see the ways this attachment causes tension and frustration inside you? Do you feel how it drives lack in your life?

6. If you can, visualize this attachment as an object you are holding in your hands. Your fingers are wrapped tightly around it.

7. Imagine what it would feel like to slowly open your fingers and let it go. Let it float away. Breathe as you do this and release control. How do you feel now?

8. Say to yourself that the future is uncertain, and you can only control what you do right now. Trust that the universe/life/God (whatever you believe in) has a bigger plan in store. Your job is to show up, do your best, and surrender the rest.

9. Come back to the present. Wiggle your toes and feel the air rushing in and out your nostrils. This is the only moment you can ever really experience – not the past, not the future, but right here, right now.

10. Stay here as long as you want, and open your eyes when you're ready to end the session.

Tips to Embody Liberation Every Day

- Speak from your heart. It's liberating to be honest and vulnerable in how you express yourself. You don't need a mask.

- Your actions and behaviors should mirror your values and beliefs.

- Love yourself as flawed as you are. Accept ALL of you without judgment or shame.

- Stop trying to control every outcome and trust the process.

- Your gut should guide your decisions, not other people's opinions.

- Be here now. This moment is all you have.

- Give without expecting anything back. Learn to be of service and contribute without needing recognition or a reward.

- Question the rules.

- The unknown is not always your enemy. Life takes unexpected twists and turns, and it'll be easier on you if you adapt and trust.

- Appreciate what you have and try not to dwell on what you think you're missing.

- Forgive yourself as willingly as you forgive others. You deserve compassion, too.

- Stay curious.

Soul Trap Exit Statement

Write down a list of affirmations that you are 100% sure will motivate you as you make your way to freedom. Recite them every day or twice a day if that's what you want. This is your journey, and how you walk it is up to you. These words will be your soul's freedom song. Scream them if you have to.

Conclusion

Can you remember how you felt before you even began chapter one? Lost? Stuck? Dissatisfied with your life in ways you can't articulate? The material world has always seemed to offer so much, hasn't it? Honestly, it's heartbreaking to learn that it is all smoke and mirrors, that the systems and structures you've been told to chase after – the six-figure careers, the fancy houses, the perpetual consumption – are nothing but distractions to keep you here while you're recycled and fed on energetically.

From the second you could form sentences, you've been trained to believe that external validation, wealth, and status are all you'll ever need to finally be complete. To have that belief system crumble will leave anyone quite disoriented for a while, but that's the fog clearing to reveal the light.

They say it is through the cracks that the light seeps in, so maybe it's time to let your long-held belief systems crack and crumble. Many people don't get this far, and you can't blame them; it's a scary place to be. The solid ground you thought you were standing on has turned to quicksand, and you don't know which way is up, but in that liminal space between the old and the new, you're born again. You become a phoenix rising powerfully from the ashes.

You are real, your light is real, and the divine is real. You're here to live a 3D life, so live it, but now you know the truth, you can see past the illusions, you see how malleable the 3D is, and that alone puts you five steps ahead of the game. You can't go back to the cave now; the light looks too good on you. Spread this light and dismantle the Matrix.

If you enjoyed this book, I'd greatly appreciate a review on Amazon because it helps me to create more books that people want. It would mean a lot to hear from you.

To leave a review:

1. Open your camera app.
2. Point your mobile device at the QR code.
3. The review page will appear in your web browser.

Thanks for your support!

Here's another book by Mari Silva that you might like

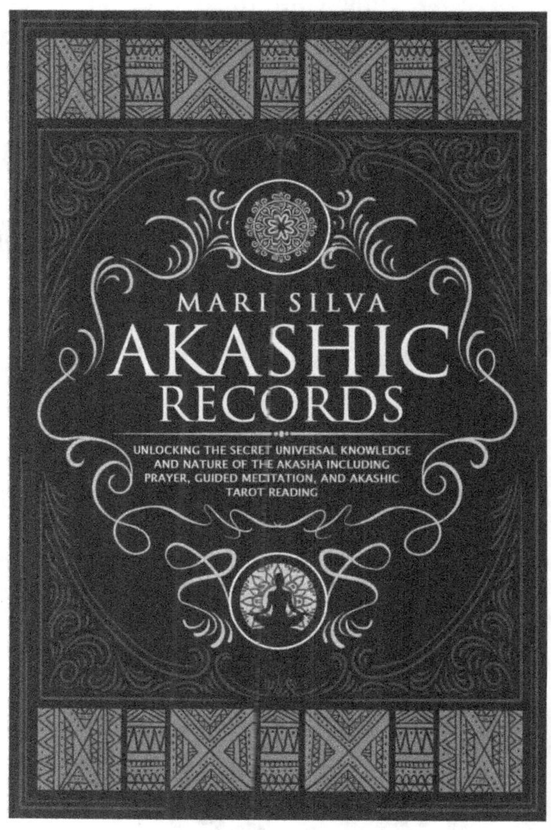

Your Free Gift
(only available for a limited time)

Thanks for getting this book! If you want to learn more about various spirituality topics, then join Mari Silva's community and get a free guided meditation MP3 for awakening your third eye. This guided meditation mp3 is designed to open and strengthen ones third eye so you can experience a higher state of consciousness. Simply visit the link below the image to get started.

https://spiritualityspot.com/meditation

Or, Scan the QR code!

References

Part 1: Soul Plan and Soul Contracts

Acharya Prashant. (2021). Karma. Penguin Enterprise.

Cayce, E. (2006). Reincarnation & karma. A.R.E. Press.

Decoz, H. (n.d.). Master Numbers in Numerology | World Numerology. Www.worldnumerology.com. https://www.worldnumerology.com/numerology-master-numbers/

DiMaggio, J. (2020). I Did It to Myself...Again! Balboa Press.

Jackson, D. (2020, August 3). Did Pythagoras invent numerology? AskAstrology. https://askastrology.com/numerology/did-pythagoras-invent-numerology/

Marlene, C. (2018, January 12). Prepare For Your Akashic Record Reading - Cheryl Marlene. Cheryl Marlene. https://www.cherylmarlene.com/prepare-for-akashic-record-reading/

Petrovic, J. (2023, August 17). Being Awakened. Being Awakened. https://www.beingawakened.com/past-life-regression/

Sloan, E. (2021). In Astrology, Each Planet Has Symbols and Meanings: Learn What They Are To Understand Your Birth Chart. Well+Good. https://www.wellandgood.com/astrology/meanings-of-planets-in-astrology

Team, T. N. (2010, February 15). The history of numerology. Numerologist.com. https://numerologist.com/numerology/the-history-of-numerology/

Tucker, J. B. (2021). Before. St. Martin's Essentials.

Wetzel, L. J. (2011). Akashic Records. Hot Pink Lotus POD.

Part 2: Soul Trap

Evers, S. (2024, December 22). *Gnosticism: The Divine Spark - Scott Evers - Medium*. Medium. https://medium.com/@scott.evers_46948/gnosticism-the-divine-spark-5f6f02304001

Freeman, M. (2015, July 22). *Soul-Catching Net – Are We "Recycled" at Death to Remain in the Matrix?* Wake up World. https://wakeup-world.com/2015/07/23/soul-catching-net-are-we-recycled-at-death-to-remain-in-the-matrix/

Instructor, G. (2020). *Liberation – Fuel for Spiritual Experience*. Glorian. https://glorian.org/learn/courses-and-lectures/fuel-for-spiritual-experience/liberation

Kadow, J. (2024, February 5). *The Power of Past Lives - Janet Kadow - Medium*. Medium. https://janetkadow.medium.com/the-power-of-past-lives-be639ca35516

McCoy, D. (n.d.). *Sophia*. Gnosticism Explained. https://gnosticismexplained.org/sophia/

McCoy, D. (2019, March 18). *The Origins of Gnosticism*. Gnosticism Explained. https://gnosticismexplained.org/the-origins-of-gnosticism/

Monte, M. (2024, January 5). *The Concept of Soul Contracts: Exploring Life's Purpose • Mind Love Podcast*. Mind Love Podcast. https://www.mindlove.com/blog/the-concept-of-soul-contracts-exploring-lifes-purpose/

Queller, K. (2023, September 24). *15 Exercises to Expand Your Intuition*. EMERGING. https://www.emergingartslife.com/post/15-exercises-to-expand-your-intuition

Regan, S. (2021, February 22). *These 7 Ancient Laws Can Help You Improve Your Life & Empower Yourself*. Mindbodygreen. https://www.mindbodygreen.com/articles/7-hermetic-principles

Trumpeter, A. (2018, August 29). *Allegory of the Cave by Plato - Summary and Meaning*. Philosophyzer. https://www.philosophyzer.com/the-allegory-of-the-cave-by-plato-summary-and-meaning/

Weiss, B. (1988). *Many Lives, Many Masters*. Piatkus.

Image Sources

1 Designed by Freepik. https://www.freepik.com/free-photo/top-view-hand-holding-
  love-letter_60249887.htm#fromView=search&page=
  3&position=10&uuid=ad80e677-dee6-4bda-aa37-
  ceb249bced5f&query=fantasy+contract

2 Photo by Justin Luebke on Unsplash https://unsplash.com/photos/person-in-yellow-
  coat-standing-on-top-of-hill-BkkVcWUgwEk

3 Rursus, CC BY-SA 3.0 <https://creativecommons.org/licenses/by-sa/3.0>, via
  Wikimedia Commons https://commons.wikimedia.org/wiki/File:Birth_chart.svg

4 Photo by Pixabay: https://www.pexels.com/photo/seven-white-closed-doors-277593/

5 Photo by Jean-Christophe André: https://www.pexels.com/photo/iceberg-2574997/

6 Designed by Pikisuperstar on Freepik. https://www.freepik.com/free-vector/modoern-
  people-doing-cultural-activities_9178339.htm#fromView=search
  &page=1&position=32&uuid=5f3a42e8-139f-4404-811a-21f67845f6ea&query=life

7 Photo by Pixabay: https://www.pexels.com/photo/group-of-people-on-street-260907/

8 Photo by Kevin Malik: https://www.pexels.com/photo/woman-sitting-on-rock-near-
  body-of-water-9032518/

9 Designed by Freepik. https://www.freepik.com/free-vector/hand-drawn-numerology-
  background_35706728.htm#fromView=search&page=1&position=0&uuid=d8ecd26f-
  151d-4fa9-ad64-1a1f0a17d308&query=numerology

10 File:Tree of life wk 02.svg: Cronholm144derivative work: נדב ס, CC BY-SA 3.0
   <https://creativecommons.org/licenses/by-sa/3.0>, via Wikimedia Commons
   https://commons.wikimedia.org/wiki/File:Tree_of_life_He_02.svg

11 Photo by Marco Milanesi: https://www.pexels.com/photo/seven-sisters-constellation-
   15586141/

12 Designed by Pikisuperstar on Freepik. https://www.freepik.com/free-vector/gradient-zodiac-sign-collection_15056777.htm#fromView=search&page=3&position=8&uuid=7eed1900-db19-4bac-9443-f8513d4ef3a0&query=zodiac+signs

13 Designed by Macrovector on Freepik. https://www.freepik.com/free-vector/solar-system-astronomy-banner_4005076.htm#fromView=search&page=1&position=3&uuid=65c0ca4d-0ab7-4f6b-a8ff-bb64919372b5&query=solar+system

14 Designed by Macrovector on Freepik. https://www.freepik.com/free-vector/horoscope-infographic-set-with-zodiac-planet-symbols-flat-vector-illustration_58574559.htm#fromView=search&page=1&position=12&uuid=3ba50d9f-7538-48e3-8794-3f9b60e5fa05&query=12+houses+astrology

15 Designed by Nikitabuida on Freepik. https://www.freepik.com/free-photo/old-russian-book_1156398.htm#fromView=search&page=1&position=24&uuid=34a97cb4-928b-4b08-bf03-f4e10cce18d0&query=magical+library

16 Photo by Pixabay: https://www.pexels.com/photo/hanging-gold-colored-pendant-with-necklace-39239/

17 Photo by Pixabay: https://www.pexels.com/photo/close-up-of-hands-257037/

18 Photo by Marcus Aurelius: https://www.pexels.com/photo/woman-practicing-yoga-6787218/

19 Photo by Pixabay: https://www.pexels.com/photo/blue-water-68474/

20 https://www.pexels.com/photo/colored-light-waves-forming-a-pattern-3121766/

21 Photo by Ron Lach : https://www.pexels.com/photo/back-view-of-a-teen-boy-with-a-digital-background-9783353/

22 Theresa Knott, CC BY-SA 3.0 <https://creativecommons.org/licenses/by-sa/3.0>, via Wikimedia Commons https://commons.wikimedia.org/wiki/File:Allegoryofthecave.svg

23 The free media repository., CC BY-SA 2.5 <https://creativecommons.org/licenses/by-sa/2.5>, via Wikimedia Commons https://commons.wikimedia.org/wiki/File:091717-34-Descartes-Philosophy.jpg

24 Photo by Vincent M.A. Janssen: https://www.pexels.com/photo/close-up-photo-of-person-wearing-guy-fawkes-mask-2698475/

25 Photo by Alexey Demidov: https://www.pexels.com/photo/a-man-looking-at-the-camera-9410494/

26 Photo by THÁI NHÀN: https://www.pexels.com/photo/monk-holding-prayer-beads-across-mountain-2730217/

27 https://openclipart.org/user-detail/xoxoxo, CC0, via Wikimedia Commons https://commons.wikimedia.org/wiki/File:Ouroboros.svg

28 Prof Ranga Sai, CC BY-SA 4.0 <https://creativecommons.org/licenses/by-sa/4.0>, via Wikimedia Commons https://commons.wikimedia.org/wiki/File:Wheel_of_Life.jpg

29 Amrkhaled 2003, CC BY-SA 4.0 <https://creativecommons.org/licenses/by-sa/4.0>, via Wikimedia Commons https://commons.wikimedia.org/wiki/File:Alexandria_library_2.jpg

30 See page for author, CC BY 4.0 <https://creativecommons.org/licenses/by/4.0>, via
Wikimedia Commons https://commons.wikimedia.org/wiki/File:
Hermes_Trismegistos,_from_Stolcius,_Viridarium_Chymicun,_1624_Wellcome_M
0011829.jpg

31 S Yao, CC BY-SA 3.0 <https://creativecommons.org/licenses/by-sa/3.0>, via
Wikimedia Commons https://commons.wikimedia.org/wiki/File:Divine_Light.JPG

32 Photo by Soumen Maity: https://www.pexels.com/photo/fire-cracker-spark-in-night-
time-photography-668254/

33 Metagignosko (Metagignosko (talk)), CC BY-SA 3.0
<https://creativecommons.org/licenses/by-sa/3.0>, via Wikimedia Commons
https://commons.wikimedia.org/wiki/File:Ecclesia_Gnostica_Holy_Sophia_
Statue.png

34 Designed by starline on Freepik. https://www.freepik.com/free-vector/digital-particle-
technology-face-artifiticial-intelligence-
concept_1586193.htm#fromView=search&page=1&position=14&uuid=df49a7fc-e10c-
4b07-8270-f232853cb285&query=human+mind

35 Photo by Pixabay: https://www.pexels.com/photo/low-section-of-man-against-sky-
247851/

36 Photo by scarlett raifur: https://www.pexels.com/photo/grayscale-photo-of-man-in-
black-suit-3869580/

37 Photo by Dziana Hasanbekava: https://www.pexels.com/photo/anonymous-woman-
walking-in-cold-field-5480739/

38 Photo by Prasanth Inturi: https://www.pexels.com/photo/silhouette-of-man-at-daytime-
1051838/

39 Photo by Isaac Taylor: https://www.pexels.com/photo/person-holding-notebook-
beside-ceramic-cup-1541216/

40 Photo by Alina Vilchenko: https://www.pexels.com/photo/woman-telling-fortune-with-
silver-pendant-7391635/

41 Designed by julos on Freepik. https://www.freepik.com/free-photo/3d-abstract-art-
brain-motion-design_47777759.htm#fromView=search&page
=1&position=10&uuid=e3b700cd-1618-4afc-9498-d2a4c556018f&query=telepathic

42 Photo by Garon Piceli: https://www.pexels.com/photo/man-wearing-white-crew-neck-
shirt-576926/

43 Mikhail Ryazanov (talk) 01:30, 1 April 2014 (UTC), CC BY-SA 3.0
<http://creativecommons.org/licenses/by-sa/3.0/>, via Wikimedia Commons
https://commons.wikimedia.org/wiki/File:Zener_cards_(color).svg

44 Photo by Alina Vilchenko: https://www.pexels.com/photo/assorted-tarot-cards-on-
table-3088369/

45 Photo by Valentin Antonucci: https://www.pexels.com/photo/person-holding-
compass-841286/

46 Photo by Alice AliNari: https://www.pexels.com/photo/woman-sitting-beside-lighted-torch-2310144/

47 Designed by pikisuperstar on Freepik. https://www.freepik.com/free-photo/full-shot-woman-with-bright-light_31590619.htm#fromView=search&page=1&position=25&uuid=610f7b03-4d6e-471b-add1-946e2b65be7c&query=reincarnation

48 Photo by Jacub Gomez: https://www.pexels.com/photo/photo-of-man-standing-on-rock-near-seashore-1142948/